# DRAMA STUDY GUIDE

# The Tragedy of Macbeth

## BY WILLIAM SHAKESPEARE

**HOLT, RINEHART AND WINSTON**
*Harcourt Brace & Company*
**Austin** • New York • Orlando • Atlanta • San Francisco • Boston • Dallas • Toronto • London

**Cover art:** Joe Melomo, Design Director; Shoehorn, Inc., Designer; Andrew Yates,
Photographer; Mike Gobbi, Photo Researcher

HRW is a registered trademark licensed to Holt, Rinehart and Winston.

Printed in the United States of America

ISBN 0-03-057322-X

5 6 7 8 9   054   09 08 07 06 05

# Contents

# INTRODUCTION

Holt, Rinehart and Winston's *Drama Study Guides* offer you and your students a rich fund of information for understanding, interpreting, and appreciating a variety of plays commonly taught in the classroom. Teachers, whether they are intimately familiar with the play or have never before taught it—perhaps not even read it—will find the Study Guide an informative, creative, and time-saving resource. Students will find that the material in each Study Guide greatly enriches their experience of the play. The Study Guide will help them respond to the plays, aid their literal comprehension, deepen their interpretations of the plays, increase their ability to recognize and respond to literary elements, stimulate their creative responses to literature, and provide them with opportunities to exercise their critical thinking skills and their writing abilities.

Each *Drama Study Guide* is designed to allow you to teach the play in the way that seems best for your students and most comfortable for you. Many sections of the Study Guide can be duplicated and then distributed to your students, either as the entire class reads a play together or as individual students or small groups of students study a particular play on their own. The materials in the Study Guide are not intended to lead to one prescribed interpretation of the play but to act as a catalyst for discussions, analyses, interpretations, conclusions, and further research.

The following are descriptions of the major sections of this Study Guide.

**Focusing on Background** Before they can fully appreciate any play, most students need some relevant background information. This section therefore supplies important information about the author's life, along with a brief discussion of his other works and philosophical orientation and comments on the play's historical context. For Shakespeare's plays the teacher is reminded of the rich background material already available in the *Elements of Literature* Pupil's and Annotated Teacher's Editions.

**Critical Responses to the Play** These comments are excerpts of critical analyses written by Shakespearean scholars. They provide interpretations of aspects of the play. Students may use this commentary as a starting point for their own interpretive essays.

**Elements of the Play** This section of the Study Guide first presents a brief outline of the play's key literary elements, which should be valuable to you as a summation of some of the elements at work in the play. It is followed by the play's cast of characters, a list that comprises summaries of the characters' roles in the plot and their relationships to one another. Next is a more detailed analysis of important elements of the play—such as theme, characterization, foreshadowing, and irony.

Some of the material in this section may be shared with students as they read the play; some will be valuable after they have read it. If students need a quick review of the definitions of literary elements, refer them to the Handbook of Literary Terms at the back of the *Elements of Literature* Pupil's Editions.

**Teaching the Play** In this section are suggestions to help you set objectives for the study of the play, introduce the drama to your class, and read the play with your entire class and with individual students. Here you will also find a section called Options for Teaching the Play, which will give you many, many practical and creative ideas for varying your instructional methods to suit the needs of particular students and particular classes.

**Plot Synopsis** The complete plot synopsis is broken down by act and scene. It is particularly useful as a timesaver and is helpful if you are teaching the play for the first time. You will probably not wish to duplicate the plot synopses for your students because students might read them instead of the play itself. You may, however, choose to share this material with students for review, reteaching, or enrichment after they have read and fully discussed the play in class.

**Guided Reading** Focusing on staging, characterization, plot development, and interpretation of action and dialogue, the questions in this section are designed to help you help students interpret the play *as they read it*. Questions correspond to specific lines in the play, and an answer or a suggested answer immediately follows each question. You may want to use these questions with students who are having difficulty with the play, giving them opportunities to follow plot and character development. Some students may find these questions useful springboards for research projects or writing assignments. If students perform parts of the play, some of these questions will help them think as directors or actors.

*Drama Study Guide: The Tragedy of Macbeth*

The following tools for instruction and assessment are provided for each act of the play or for selected acts. This material is presented in the form of worksheets, questions, and activities, all of which may be duplicated for student's use.

The exercises in the **Graphic Organizer for Active Reading** give students the opportunity to record responses and organize their ideas before and/or after they read each act of the play.

**Making Meanings** opens with literal recall questions (Reviewing the Text) and then moves on to questions calling for higher-level thinking skills, including responding to the text, inferential thinking, generalizing, predicting, extending the text, and even challenging the text. Following Act V are Making Meanings questions that require students to make informed judgments about the play as a whole by drawing on their skills of analysis, synthesis, and evaluation.

Making Meanings questions are designed for maximum flexibility. These questions, which are provided for each act of the play, may be distributed to students prior to their reading of an act so that they can read it with more focus. The questions may also be used for classroom discussion. Alternatively, they may be answered in writing as homework or as an in-class assignments.

Students should be encouraged to respond to at least some of the Making Meanings questions in writing even if you use these questions primarily as a basis for classroom discussion. Students may then record their answers in a journal or a reading log—a notebook of creative, critical, and emotional responses that they record as they read the text. Students may share, and use interactively, material from these notebooks with one another and/or with you.

A **How to Own a Word Mini-Lesson,** included for Act V, offers students strategies for making Shakespeare's vocabulary part of their own.

A **Words to Own Worksheet,** included for one act of the play, offers exercises using words from the play.

A **Language and Style Mini-Lesson,** included for one act of the play, focuses on aspects of Shakespeare's verse.

**Language Link Worksheets,** included for selected acts, offer a hands-on approach to an understanding of specific elements of Shakespeare's style.

An **Elements of Literature Mini-Lesson,** included for Act V, focuses on the play's imagery and figurative language.

**Literary Elements Worksheets,** provided for each act, identify key literary elements in the play. Each worksheet gives students exercises to test their recognition and understanding of these elements.

**Choices: Building Your Portfolio** is a collection of critical and creative assignments that call for writing, research, performance, and artwork. Creative writing assignments extend the play to new territory. For example, an assignment may ask students to retell an important episode or rewrite the ending of the play in their own words. It may ask them to write an imagined sequel to the play or to cast appropriate contemporary actors in the roles of the play's main characters. All these assignments enable students to demonstrate creatively their understanding of the play. Critical writing assignments ask students to respond to the play through a critical-analytical route. For example, an assignment may ask students to respond to a critic's comments about the play, supporting or refuting those comments using specific evidence from the play. It may ask them to compare and contrast two characters in the play or to demonstrate how a theme of the play is captured in a recurring symbol.

Choices activities also suggest research projects and assignments in drama, art, and music that take the student beyond the play itself and allow you to make valuable cross-curriculum connections.

**Tests,** reproducible for classroom use, are provided for each act. They include objective questions that are based on recall of key events in the plot, questions that require an analysis of literary elements, and short essay questions that cover the interpretation, evaluation, and analysis of the play.

There is also a **Test** for the play as a whole and one for **Testing the Genre.**

An **English Language Worksheet** consists of objective questions about Shakespeare's language.

**Cross-Curricular Activity** This interdisciplinary, theme-based activity is appropriate for team teaching.

**Read On** This section is included for teachers and students who wish to extend their reading. It lists works by other writers that use topics or themes connected with the play.

**Answer Key** The Answer Key is complete, providing answers to objective questions as well as to interpretive questions, to which there is no one correct answer. In the latter case, several possible responses may be suggested.

# Focusing on Background

## The Life and Work of William Shakespeare (1564–1616)

*by* **C. F. Main**    C. F. Main was for many years a professor of English at Rutgers University in New Brunswick, New Jersey. He is the editor of *Poems: Wadsworth Handbook and Anthology* and has written reviews and articles on sixteenth-, seventeenth-, and eighteenth-century literature.

Every literate person has heard of William Shakespeare, the author of more than three dozen remarkable plays and more than 150 poems. Over the centuries these literary works have made such a deep impression on the human race that all sorts of fancies, legends, and theories have been invented about their author. There are even those who say that somebody other than Shakespeare wrote the works that bear his name, although these deluded people cannot agree on who, among a dozen candidates, this other author actually was. Such speculation is based on the wrong assumption that little is known about Shakespeare's life; in fact, Shakespeare's life is better documented than the life of any other dramatist of the time except perhaps Ben Jonson, a writer who seems almost modern in the way he publicized himself. Jonson was an honest, blunt, and outspoken man who knew Shakespeare well; for a time the two dramatists wrote for the same theatrical company, and Shakespeare even acted in Jonson's plays. Often ungenerous in his praise of other writers, Jonson published a poem asserting that Shakespeare was superior to all Greek, Roman, and other English dramatists and predicting that he would be "not of an age, but for all time." Jonson's judgment is now commonly accepted, and his prophecy has come true.

Shakespeare was born in Stratford-on-Avon, a historic and prosperous market town in Warwickshire, and was christened in the parish church there on April 26, 1564. His father was John Shakespeare, a merchant at one time active in the town government; his mother—born Mary Arden—came from a prominent family in the country. For seven years or so William attended the Stratford Grammar School, where he obtained an excellent education in Latin, the Bible, and English composition. (The students had to write out English translations of Latin works and then turn them back into Latin.) After leaving school, he may have been apprenticed to a butcher, but because he shows in his plays very detailed knowledge of many different crafts and trades, scholars have proposed a number of different occupations that he could have followed. At eighteen, Shakespeare married Anne Hathaway, the twenty-seven-year-old daughter of a farmer living near Stratford. They had three children, a daughter named Susanna and twins named Hamnet and Judith. We don't know how the young Shakespeare supported his family, but according to tradition he taught school for a few years. The two daughters grew up and married; the son died when he was eleven.

How did Shakespeare first become interested in the theater? Presumably by seeing plays. We know that traveling acting companies frequently visited Stratford, and we assume that he attended their performances and that he also went to the nearby city of Coventry, where a famous cycle of religious plays was put on every year. But to be a dramatist, one had to be in London, where the theater was flourishing in the 1580s. Just when Shakespeare left his family and moved to London (there is no evidence that his wife was ever in the city) is uncertain; scholars say that he arrived there in 1587 or 1588. It is certain that he was busy and successful in the London theater by 1592, when a fellow dramatist named Robert Greene attacked him in print and ridiculed a passage in his early play *Henry VI*. Greene, a down-and-out Cambridge graduate, warned other university men then writing plays to beware of this "upstart crow beautified with our feathers." Greene died of dissipation just as his ill-natured attack was being published, but a friend of his named Henry Chettle immediately apologized in print to Shakespeare and commended Shakespeare's acting and writing ability, and his personal honesty.

From 1592 on, there is ample documentation of Shakespeare's life and works. We know where he lived in London, at least approximately when his plays were produced and printed, and even how he spent his money. From 1594 to his retirement in about 1613, he was continuously a member of one company, which also included the great tragic actor Richard Burbage and the popular clown Will Kemp. Although actors and others connected with the theater had a very low status legally, in practice they enjoyed the patronage of noblemen and even royalty. It is a mistake to think of Shakespeare as an obscure actor who somehow wrote great plays; he was well-known even as a young man. He first became famous as the author of a best-seller, an erotic narrative poem called *Venus and Adonis* (1593). This poem, as well as a more serious one entitled *Lucrece* (1594), was dedicated to a rich and extravagant young nobleman, the earl of Southampton. The dedication of *Lucrece* suggests that Shakespeare and his patron were on very friendly terms.

## Shakespeare's Early Plays

Among Shakespeare's earliest plays are the following, with the generally but not universally accepted dates of their first performance: *Richard III* (1592–1593), a "chronicle," or history, about a deformed usurper who became king of England; *The Comedy of Errors* (1592–1593), a rowdy farce of mistaken identity based on a Latin play; *Titus Andronicus* (1593–1594), a blood-and-thunder tragedy full of rant and atrocities; *The Taming of the Shrew* (1593–1594), *The Two Gentlemen of Verona* (1593–1595), and *Love's Labor's Lost* (1593–1594), three agreeable comedies; and *Romeo and Juliet* (1594–1595), a poetic tragedy of ill-fated lovers. The extraordinary thing about these plays is not so much their immense variety— each one is quite different from all the others—but the fact that they are all regularly revived and performed on stages all over the world today.

By 1596, Shakespeare was beginning to prosper. He had his father apply to the Heralds' College for a coat of arms that the family could display, signifying that they were "gentlefolks." On Shakespeare's family crest a falcon is shown, shaking a spear. To support this claim to gentility, Shakespeare bought New Place, a handsome house and grounds in Stratford, a place so commodious and elegant that the queen of England once stayed there after Shakespeare's daughter Susanna inherited it. Shakespeare also, in 1599, joined with a few other members of his company, now called the Lord Chamberlain's Men, to finance a new theater on the south side of the Thames—the famous Globe. The "honey-tongued Shakespeare," as he was called in a book about English literature published in 1598, was now earning money as a playwright, an actor, and a shareholder in a theater. By 1600, Shakespeare was regularly associating with members of the aristocracy, and six of his plays had been given command performances at the court of Queen Elizabeth.

During the last years of Elizabeth I's reign, Shakespeare completed his cycle of plays about England during the Wars of the Roses: *Richard II* (1595–1596), both parts of *Henry IV* (1597–1598), and *Henry V* (1599–1600). Also in this period he wrote the play most frequently studied in schools—*Julius Caesar* (1599–1600)—and the comedies that are most frequently performed today: *A Midsummer Night's Dream* (1595–1596), *The Merchant of Venice* (1596–1597), *Much Ado About Nothing* (1598–1599), and *As You Like It* and *Twelfth Night* (1599–1600). And finally at this time he wrote or rewrote *Hamlet* (1600–1601), the tragedy that, of all his tragedies, has provoked the most varied and controversial interpretations from critics, scholars, and actors.

Shakespeare indeed prospered under Queen Elizabeth; according to an old tradition, she asked him to write *The Merry Wives of Windsor* (1600–1601) because she wanted to see the merry, fat old knight Sir John Falstaff (of the *Henry* plays) in love.

He prospered even more under Elizabeth's successor, King James of Scotland. Fortunately for Shakespeare's company, as it turned out, James's royal entry into London in 1603 had to be postponed for several months because the plague was raging in the city. While waiting for the epidemic to subside, the royal court stayed in various palaces outside London. Shakespeare's company took advantage of this situation and, since the city theaters were closed, performed several plays for the court and the new king. Shakespeare's plays delighted James, for he loved literature and was starved for pleasure after the grim experience of ruling Scotland for many years. He immediately took the company under his patronage, renamed them the King's Men, gave them patents to perform anywhere in the realm, provided them with special clothing for state occasions, increased their salaries, and appointed their chief members, including Shakespeare, to be grooms of the Royal Chamber. All this patronage brought such prosperity to Shakespeare that he was able to make some very profitable real estate investments in Stratford and London.

## Shakespeare's "Tragic Period"

In the early years of the seventeenth century, while his financial affairs were flourishing and everything was apparently going very well for Shakespeare, he wrote his greatest tragedies: *Hamlet* (already mentioned), *Othello* (1604–1605), *King Lear* (1605–1606), *Macbeth* (1605–1606), and *Antony and Cleopatra* (1606–1607). Because these famous plays are so preoccupied with evil, violence, and death, some people feel that Shakespeare must have been very unhappy and depressed when he wrote them. Moreover, such people find even the comedies he wrote at this time more sour than sweet: *Troilus and Cressida* (1601–1603), *All's Well That*

*Ends Well* (1602–1603), and *Measure for Measure* (1604–1605). And so, instead of paying tribute to Shakespeare's powerful imagination, which is everywhere evident, these people invent a "tragic period" in Shakespeare's biography, and they search for personal crises in his private life. When they cannot find these agonies, they invent them. To be sure, in 1607 an actor named Edward Shakespeare, who may well have been William's younger brother, died in London. But by 1607 Shakespeare's alleged "tragic period" was almost over!

It is quite wrong to assume a one-to-one correspondence between writers' lives and their works, because writers must be allowed to imagine whatever they can. It is especially wrong in the case of a writer like Shakespeare, who did not write to express himself but to satisfy the patrons of the theater that he and his partners owned. Shakespeare must have repeatedly given the audience just what it wanted; otherwise, he could not have made so much money out of the theater. To insist that he had to experience and feel personally everything that he wrote about is absurd. He wrote about King Lear, who cursed his two monstrous daughters for treating him very badly; in contrast, what evidence there is suggests that he got along very well with his own two daughters. And so, instead of "tragic," we should think of the years 1600–1607 as glorious, because in them Shakespeare's productivity was at its peak. It seems very doubtful that a depressed person would write plays like these. In fact, they would make their creator feel exhilarated rather than sad.

## The Last Years

In 1612, Shakespeare decided that, having made a considerable sum from his plays and theatrical enterprises, he would retire to his handsome house in Stratford, a place he had never forgotten, though he seems to have kept his life there rather separate from his life in London. His retirement was not complete, for the records show that after he returned to Stratford, he still took part in the management of the King's Men and their two theaters: the Globe, a polygonal building opened in 1599 and used for performances in good weather, and the Blackfriars, acquired in 1608 and used for indoor performances. Shakespeare's works in this period show no signs of diminished creativity, except that in some years he wrote one play instead of the customary two, and they continue to illustrate the great diversity of his genius. Among them are the tragedies *Timon of Athens* (1607–1608) and *Coriolanus* (1607–1608) and five plays that have been variously classified as comedies, romances, or tragicomedies; *Pericles* (1608–1609), *Cymbeline* (1609–1610), *The Winter's Tale* (1610–1611),

*The Tempest* (1611–1612), and *The Two Noble Kinsmen* (1612–1613). His last English history play, *Henry VIII* (1612–1613), contains a tribute to Queen Elizabeth—a somewhat tardy tribute, because, unlike most of the other poets of the day, Shakespeare did not praise her in print when she died in 1603. (Some scholars argue, on very little evidence, that he was an admirer of the earl of Essex, a former intimate of Elizabeth's whom she had beheaded for rebelliousness.) During the first performance of *Henry VIII,* in June of 1613, the firing of the cannon at the end of Act I set the Globe on fire (it had a thatched roof), and it burned to the ground. Only one casualty is recorded; a bottle of ale had to be poured on a man whose breeches were burning. Fortunately, the company had the Blackfriars in which to perform until the Globe could be rebuilt and reopened in 1614.

Shakespeare's last recorded visit to London, accompanied by his son-in-law Dr. John Hall, was in November 1614, though he may have gone down to the city afterward because he continued to own property there, including a building very near the Blackfriars Theater. Probably, though, he spent most of the last two years of his life at New Place, with his daughter Susanna Hall (and his granddaughter Elizabeth) living nearby. He died on April 23, 1616, and was buried under the floor of Stratford Church, with this epitaph warning posterity not to dig him up and transfer him to the graveyard outside the church—a common practice in those days when space was needed:

> Good friend, for Jesus' sake forbear
> To dig the bones enclosèd here!
> Blest be the man that spares these stones,
> And curst be he that moves my bones.

## Shakespeare's Genius

What sort of man was Shakespeare? This is a very hard question to answer because he left no letters, diaries, or other private writings containing his personal views; instead, he left us plays, and in a good play the actors do not speak for the dramatist but for the characters they are impersonating. We cannot, then, say that Shakespeare approved of evil because he created murderers or advocated religion because he created clergymen; we cannot say that he believed in fatalism because he created fatalists or admired flattery because he created flatterers. All these would be naive, and contradictory, reactions to the plays. Shakespeare's characters represent such a vast range of human behavior and attitudes that they must be products of his careful observation and fertile imagination rather than extensions of himself. A critic named Desmond McCarthy once said that trying to identify Shakespeare the man in his plays is like looking at a very dim portrait under glass: The more you peer at it, the more you see only yourself.

One thing is certain: Shakespeare was a complete man of the theater who created works specifically for his own acting company and his own stage. He had, for instance, to provide good parts in every play for the principal performers in the company, including the comedians acting in tragedies. Since there were no actresses, he had to limit the number of female parts in his plays and create them in such a way that they could readily be taken by boys. For instance, although there are many fathers in the plays, there are very few mothers: While boys could be taught to flirt and play shy, acting maternally would be difficult for them. Several of Shakespeare's young women disguise themselves as young men early in Act I—an easy solution to the problem of boys playing girls' parts. Shakespeare also had to provide the words for songs because theatergoers expected singing in every play; furthermore, the songs had to be devised so that they would exhibit the talents of particular actors with good voices. Since many of the plays contain many characters, and since there were a limited number of actors in the company, Shakespeare had to arrange for doubling and even tripling of roles; that is, a single actor would have to perform more than one part. Since, of course, an actor could impersonate only one character at a time, Shakespeare had to plan his scenes carefully, so that nobody would ever have to be onstage in two different roles at the same time. A careful study of the plays shows that Shakespeare handled all these technical problems of dramaturgy very masterfully.

Although the plays are primarily performance scripts, from earliest times the public has wanted to read them as well as see them staged. In every gen-eration, people have felt that the plays contain so much wisdom, so much knowledge of human nature, so much remarkable poetry, that they need to be pondered in private as well as enjoyed in public. Most readers have agreed with what the poet John Dryden said about Shakespeare's "soul": The man who wrote the plays may be elusive, but he was obviously a great genius whose lofty imagination is matched by his sympathy for all kinds of human behavior. Reading the plays, then, is a rewarding experience in itself; it is also an excellent preparation for seeing them performed onstage or on film.

Shakespeare's contemporaries were so eager to read his plays that enterprising publishers did everything possible, including stealing them, to make them available. Of course the company generally tried to keep the plays unpublished because they did not want them performed by rival companies. Even so, eighteen plays were published in small books, called quartos, before Shakespeare's partners collected them and published them after his death. This collection, known as the first folio because of its large size, was published in 1623. Surviving copies of this folio are regarded as valuable treasures today. But, of course, the general reader need not consult any of the original texts of Shakespeare because his works never go out of print; they are always available in many different languages and many different formats. The plays that exist in two different versions (one in a quarto and one in the folio) have provided scholars with endless matter for speculation about what Shakespeare actually intended the correct text to be. Indeed, every aspect of Shakespeare has been, and continues to be, thoroughly studied and written about, by literary and historical scholars, by theater and film people, by experts in many fields, and by amateurs of every stripe. No wonder that he is mistakenly regarded as a great mystery.

# The Renaissance Theater
*by* **C. F. Main**

By the mid-sixteenth century, the art of drama in England was three centuries old, but the idea of housing it in a permanent building was new, and even after theaters had been built, plays were still regularly performed in improvised spaces when acting companies were touring the provinces or presenting their plays in the large houses of royalty and nobility.

In 1576, James Burbage, the father of Shakespeare's partner and fellow actor Richard Burbage, built the first public theater and called it, appropriately, the Theater. Shortly thereafter, a second playhouse, called the Curtain, was erected. Both of these were located in a northern suburb of London, where they would not affront the more staid and sober-minded residents of London proper. Then came the Rose, the Swan, the Fortune, the Globe, the Red Bull, and the Hope: an astonishing number of public theaters and far more than there were in any other capital city of Europe at that time.

# The Globe

The Globe, of course, is the most famous of these because it was owned by the company which Shakespeare belonged to. It was built out of timbers salvaged from the Theater when the latter was demolished in 1599. These timbers were carted across London, rafted over the Thames, and re-assembled on the Bankside near a beer garden—not the most elegant of London suburbs. Since many of Shakespeare's plays received their first performances in the Globe, curiosity and speculation about this famous building have been common for the last two hundred years or more. Unfortunately, the plans for the Globe have not survived, though there still exist old panoramic drawings of London in which its exterior is pictured, and there is still considerable information available about some other theaters, including a sketch of the Swan's stage and the building contract for the Fortune. But the most important sources of information are the plays themselves, with their stage directions and other clues to the structure of the theater.

## The Structure of the Globe

At the present time most scholars accept as accurate the reconstruction of the Globe published by the contemporary British author C. Walter Hodges. The theater has three main parts: the building proper, the stage, and the tiring house (or backstage area), with a flag that flew from its peak whenever there was to be a performance that day.

The theater building proper was a wooden structure three stories high surrounding a spacious inner yard open to the sky. It was probably a sixteen-sided polygon. Any structure with that many sides would appear circular, so it is not surprising that Shakespeare referred to the Globe as "the wooden O" in his play *Henry V.* There were probably only two entrances to the building, one for the public and one for the theater company, but there may well have been another public door used as an exit, because when the Globe burned down in 1613, the crowd escaped the flames quickly and safely. General admission to the theater cost one penny; this entitled a spectator to be a groundling, which meant he or she could stand in the yard. Patrons paid a little more to mount up into the galleries, where there were seats and where there was a better view of the stage, along its two sides; people who wanted to be conspicuous rented them, and they must have been a great nuisance to the rest of the audience and the actors. A public theater could hold a surprisingly large number of spectators: three thousand, according to two different contemporary accounts. The spectators must have been squeezed together, and so it is no wonder that the authorities always closed the theaters during epidemics of plague. The stage jutted halfway out into the yard so that the actors were in much closer contact with the audience than they are in modern theaters, most of which have picture-frame stages with orchestra pit, proscenium arch, and front curtains. A picture-frame stage usually attempts to give the illusion of reality: Its painted scenery represents the walls of a room or an outdoor vista, and the actors pretend that nobody is watching them perform, at least until it is time to take a bow. To be sure, theater designs have been changing since World War II, and people have again learned to enjoy plays "in the round," without elaborate realistic settings. Modern audiences are learning to accept what Renaissance audiences took for granted: that the theater cannot show reality. Whatever happens on the stage is make-believe. Spectators at the Globe loved to see witches or devils emerge through the trapdoor in the stage, which everybody pretended led down to hell, though everybody knew that it did not, just as everybody knew that the ceiling over part of the stage was not really the heavens. This ceiling was painted with elaborate suns, moons, and stars, and it contained a trapdoor through which angels, gods, and spirits could be lowered on a wire and even flown over the other actors' heads. Such large sensational effects as these were plentiful in the Renaissance theater. At the opposite extreme, every tiny nuance of an individual actor's performance could affect the audience, which was also very close to the stage. The actors were highly trained, and they could sing, dance, declaim, wrestle, fence, clown, roar, weep, and whisper. Unfortunately, none of this liveliness can be conveyed by the printed page; we must imagine all the activity onstage as we read.

The third structural element in this theater was the tiring house, a tall building that contained machinery and dressing rooms and that provided a two-story back wall for the stage. Hodge's drawing shows that this wall contained a gallery above and a curtained space below. The gallery had multiple purposes, depending on what play was being performed. Spectators could sit there, musicians could perform there, or parts of the play could be acted there. Many plays have stage directions indicating that some actors should appear on a level above the other actors—on the balconies, towers, city walls, parapets, fortifications, hills, and the like. The curtained area below the gallery was used mainly for "discoveries" of things prepared in advance and temporarily kept hidden from the audience until the proper times for showing them. In Shakespeare's *Merchant of Venice,* for example, the curtain is drawn to reveal (or "discover") three

*Drama Study Guide: The Tragedy of Macbeth*

HRW MATERIAL COPYRIGHTED UNDER NOTICE APPEARING EARLIER IN THIS WORK.

7

small chests, in one of which is hidden the heroine's picture. Some modern accounts of Renaissance theaters refer to this curtained area as an inner stage, but apparently it was too small, too shallow, and too far out of the sight of some spectators to be used as a performance space. If a performer were "discovered" behind the curtains, as Marlowe's Dr. Faustus is discovered in his study with his books, he would quickly move out onto the stage to be better seen and heard. Thrones, banquets, beds, writing desks, and so on could be pushed through the curtains onto the stage, and as soon as a large property of this sort appeared, the audience would know at once that the action was taking place indoors. When the action shifted to the outdoors, the property could be pulled back behind the curtain.

## Scenery

The people in the audience were quite prepared to use their imaginations. When they saw actors carrying lanterns, they knew it was night even though the sun was shining brightly overhead. Often, instead of seeing a scene, they heard it described, as when a character exclaims,

> But look, the morn in russet mantle clad,
> Walks o'er the dew of yon high eastward hill.
> —*Hamlet,*
> Act I, Scene 1

Shakespeare could not show a sunrise; instead of trying to, he wrote a speech inviting the audience to imagine one. When the stage had to become a forest, as in several of Shakespeare's comedies, there was no painted scenery trying (and usually failing) to look like real trees, bushes, flowers, and so on. Instead, a few bushes and small trees might be pushed onto the stage, and then the actors created the rest of the scenery by speaking poetry that evoked images in the spectators' minds. In *As You Like It,* Rosalind simply looks around her and announces "Well, this is the Forest of Arden."

The great advantage of this theater was its speed and flexibility. The stage could be anywhere, and the play did not have to be interrupted while the sets were shifted. By listening to what was being said, the audience learned all that they needed to know about where the action was taking place at any given moment; they did not need to consult a printed program.

## Act and Scene Divisions

Most of the act and scene divisions in Renaissance drama have been added by later editors, who have tried to adapt plays written for the old platform stage to the modern picture-frame stage. In this process,

editors have badly damaged one play in particular, Shakespeare's *Antony and Cleopatra.* This play was published and republished for a hundred years after Shakespeare's death without any act and scene divisions at all. Then one editor cut it up into twenty-seven different scenes, and another into forty-four, thus better suiting the play to the picture-frame stage, or so they thought. But a stage manager would go mad trying to provide realistic scenery for this many different locales. Even a reader becomes confused and irritated trying to imagine all the different places where the characters are going according to the modern stage directions, which are of a kind that Shakespeare and his contemporaries never heard of. "Theirs was a drama of persons, not a drama of places," according to Gerald Bentley, one of our best theatrical historians.

## Props and Effects

Some modern accounts have overemphasized the bareness of Renaissance theaters; actually they were ornate rather than bare. Their interiors were painted brightly, there were many decorations, and the space at the rear of the stage could be covered with colorful tapestries or hangings. Costumes were rich, elaborate, and expensive. The manager-producer Philip Henslowe, whose account books preserve much important information about the early theater, once paid twenty pounds, then an enormous sum, for a single cloak for one of his actors to wear in a play. Henslowe's lists of theatrical properties mention, among other things, chariots, fountains, dragons, beds, tents, thrones, booths, wayside crosses. The audience enjoyed the processions—religious, royal, military—that occur in many plays. These would enter the stage from one door, pass over the stage, and then exit by the other door. A few quick costume changes in the tiring house, as the actors passed through, could double and triple the number of people in a procession. Pageantry, sound effects, music both vocal and instrumental—all these elements helped give the audience their money's worth of theatrical experience.

## Private Halls and Indoor Theaters

These, then, were the chief features of the public theaters that Renaissance dramatists had to keep in mind as they wrote their plays. In addition to these theaters, the acting companies also performed in two other kinds of spaces: in the great halls of castles and manor houses and in certain indoor theaters in London (which are called indoor theaters to distinguish them from theaters like the Globe, which were only partly roofed over).

*Drama Study Guide: The Tragedy of Macbeth*

For performances in a great hall, a theater company must have had a portable booth stage, a building where the usual entertainment was a bear being attacked by dogs. The bear pits were vile places, but the temporary stages set up in them could easily accommodate any play written for the public theater except for scenes requiring the use of heavens overhanging the stage.

Something like this booth stage may also have been used in the private theaters like the Blackfriars, which Shakespeare's company, the King's Men, acquired in 1608. Although nothing is known about the physical features of the Blackfriars stage, we know that the building itself—a disused monastery—was entirely roofed over, unlike the Globe, where only part of the stage and part of the audience had the protection of a roof. One great advantage of Blackfriars was that the company could perform there in cold weather and, since artificial lighting always had to be used, at night. And so the King's Men could put on plays all during the year, with increased profits for the shareholders, among them Shakespeare.

## Shakespeare's Plays

*Henry VI*, Part II (1590–1591)
*Henry VI*, Part III (1590–1591)
*Henry VI*, Part I (1591–1592)
*The Comedy of Errors* (1592–1593)
*Richard III* (1592–1593)
*Titus Andronicus* (1593–1594)
*The Taming of the Shrew* (1593–1594)
*Love's Labor's Lost* (1593–1594)
*The Two Gentlemen of Verona* (1593–1595)
*Romeo and Juliet* (1594–1595)
*Richard II* (1595–1596)
*A Midsummer Night's Dream* (1595–1596)
*King John* (1596–1597)
*The Merchant of Venice* (1596–1597)
*Henry IV*, Part I (1597)
*Henry IV*, Part II (1597–1598)
*Much Ado About Nothing* (1598–1599)
*Henry V* (1599–1600)
*Julius Caesar* (1599–1600)

*As You Like It* (1599–1600)
*Twelfth Night* (1599–1600)
*Hamlet* (1600–1601)
*The Merry Wives of Windsor* (1600–1601)
*Troilus and Cressida* (1601–1603)
*All's Well That Ends Well* (1602–1603)
*Othello* (1604–1605)
*Measure for Measure* (1604–1605)
*King Lear* (1605–1606)
*Macbeth* (1605–1606)
*Antony and Cleopatra* (1606–1607)
*Timon of Athens* (1607–1608)
*Coriolanus* (1607–1608)
*Pericles* (1608–1609)
*Cymbeline* (1609–1610)
*The Winter's Tale* (1610–1611)
*The Tempest* (1611–1612)
*The Two Noble Kinsmen* (1612–1613)
*Henry VIII* (1612–1613)

## Sources for *The Tragedy of Macbeth*

*by* **Sylvan Barnet**

Literature commonly has two sources: It owes something to the thoughts and activities of the day, and it owes much to earlier literature. *Macbeth* is no exception.

First, *Macbeth* is indebted to the fact that a Scot had acceded to the English throne. More specifically, James I had written a book called *Demonology,* and in it Shakespeare could have learned, for example, that witches can foretell the future. If Shakespeare wanted to please or honor James, who was supposedly descended from Ban-

quo, he would naturally write a play about Scottish history showing James's ancestor in a favorable light and making use of James's interest in witchcraft. Yet another, though smaller, influence of the age is seen in the discussion of equivocation in Act II, Scene 3, a topic much in the air after the trial of the Jesuit father Garnett (March 1606), who had admitted that he believed equivocation was justifiable if used for a good end.

If we turn to books, it is evident that Shakespeare's chief debt is to Holinshed's *Chronicles of*

*England, Scotlande, and Irelande* [1577]. In Holinshed, Shakespeare found not only the story of Macbeth, who killed King Duncan, but another story of regicide that suited his purposes even better. Holinshed says that Duncan was "negligent" and that during his reign "many misruled persons took occasion thereof to trouble the peace and quiet state of the commonwealth." According to the *Chronicles,* Macbeth, with Banquo, openly killed the king; Macbeth's wife is mentioned only once. Shakespeare, clearly, had to dissociate Banquo from Macbeth and perhaps give Macbeth some other ally. He found a way in Holinshed's story of Donwald, who, urged by his wife, killed his guest, the pious King Duff. But even the story of Donwald and his wife did not contain the sleepwalking scene that Shakespeare invented for Lady Macbeth. A study of the episodes in Holinshed shows that Holinshed actually provided only the broad outline of the story and some hints for particular episodes rather than the characters as we know them or the moral feeling as we sense it.

Other books provided some additional material: Possibly Shakespeare browsed through several works on witchcraft and on Scottish history; possibly Seneca's *Agamemnon* helped him (in its portrait of Clytemnestra) to draw Lady Macbeth; certainly *Agamemnon* gave him a few verbal tags, as did the Bible, which also gave him, more important, a conception of the consequences of sin. Finally, it should be mentioned that Shakespeare, like other writers, borrowed from himself. Macbeth owes something to Tarquin in *Lucrece,* who at night performs a deed he knows is repellent and who is aware of his shortsightedness in giving up what Macbeth calls his "eternal jewel":

Who buys a minute's mirth to wail a week?
Or sells eternity to get a toy?
—*The Rape of Lucrece,* lines 213–214

# Critical Responses to *The Tragedy of Macbeth*

## "Thou Shalt Not Kill"
*from* an Introduction to *The Tragedy of Macbeth*

*by* **Alfred Harbage**

*Macbeth* is the shortest of Shakespeare's tragedies and the simplest in its statement: *Thou shalt not kill.* In the words of Coleridge, it contains "no reasonings of equivocal morality, . . . no sophistry of self-delusion." With eyes wide open to the hideousness of his offense, a brave, imaginative, and morally sensitive man commits a stealthy murder for gain. His victim is his guest, his benefactor, his kinsman, and his king; and to shield himself from detection, he incontinently sacrifices the lives and reputation of two innocent underlings. The retribution is as appalling as the crime—his soul's slow death in self-horror, degradation, loneliness, and despair, then his bloody extermination.

Why should such a man do such evil? That we ask the question instead of dismissing the play as an incredible fiction is our tribute to the poet's vision and artistry. The question reshapes itself on our lips: Why is there evil for men to do? And we realize that there can be no answer. The core of *Macbeth* is a religious mystery, its moral clarity a testament of faith. Evil may be recognized, loathed, and combated without being understood: "In these matters we still have judgment here."

The earliest mention of the play occurs in notes on a performance at the Globe, April 10, 1611, by the spectator Simon Forman, but the style and a few shreds of literary evidence suggest 1605–1606 as the period of composition; hence it followed *Hamlet, Othello,* and possibly also *Lear,* those other tragedies in which destruction is wrought by naked evil, not mere domestic or political strife. *Macbeth* differs from the other three in that the evil works through the protagonist as well as upon him. The one with whom we identify is the one who is possessed; this citadel crumbles from within. The supernatural soliciting of the weird sisters, the strenuous persuasions of the wife, do not explain Macbeth's guilt. They enhance its power over our imagination by revealing stages in its course and suggesting forces in perilous balance.

In Holinshed's *Chronicle,* from which Shakespeare drew his material, adding to the sins of the semi-legendary Macbeth those of Donwald, slayer of King Duff, the weird sisters are "goddesses of destinie" derived from a heathen fatalism. In the play they are Elizabethan witches, their prescriptive powers subtly curtailed; they predict, abet, and symbolize damnation but do not determine it. Any sense that Macbeth is a helpless victim, his crime predestined, his will bound, is canceled as the play proceeds. We may seem to see in the encounter on the heath the very inception of his lethal designs. But we should ask with Banquo,

> Good sir, why do you start, and seem to fear
> Things that do sound so fair?

Nothing in the witches' prophecies would have suggested to an untainted mind that to "be king hereafter" meant to be murderer first. That Macbeth was already tainted would have been apparent to the original audience. In another play of the era, *The Witch of Edmonton,* the black dog appears at her side only when the wish for his presence is wrung from old Mother Sawyer's lips. The stars could influence but could not govern, the devils could come but only upon summons. At some unknown time for some unknown reason, Macbeth has corrupted in pride and has contemplated the sale of his soul as certainly as Faustus. When we later discover through the words of his lady that plans to murder Duncan had preceded the meeting on the heath, we should not bring charges of inconsistency, speculate about "lost scenes," or complain that we have been tricked.

The prophecies, nevertheless, without explaining or excusing Macbeth's crimes, impress us as mitigation: Powerful and wily forces are speeding him on his course. The more earthly influence of his lady's persuasions impresses us in a similar way. They provide, moreover, an occasion for the display of his aversion for what he is about to do and convert it, at least in some measure, from utter self-serving into an offering to her. Lady Macbeth's own behavior is not totally alienating. In a perverted way she is doing what all loyal wives are expected to do, urging her husband on to what she deems his good; here, as in the period of danger that follows, she at least is *all for him.* This is one of the marvels of the play, the manner in which this frightful collusion proceeds in an atmosphere of domestic virtue without the effect of irony. If the evil is great, it is also limited, even in respect to the malefactors. After the lady's collapse, her initial ferocity is remembered as something false to her nature, and the solicitude of her wise and kindly physician seems to us not misplaced.

Macbeth himself is as humane in his reflections as he is inhumane in his acts, . . . but his moralizing is not clever aphoristic display. It comes from his heart, sometimes like an echo of ancient folk beliefs,

It will have blood, they say: blood will have
    blood.
Stones have been known to move and trees to
    speak;
Augurs and understood relations have
By maggot-pies and choughs and rooks
    brought forth
The secret'st man of blood.

Sometimes like religious revelation,

. . . [Duncan's] virtues
Will plead like angels trumpet-tongued against
The deep damnation of his taking-off;
And pity, like a naked newborn babe,
Striding the blast, or heaven's cherubin horsed
Upon the sightless couriers of the air,
Shall blow the horrid deed in every eye,
That tears shall drown the wind.

No voice in literature has sounded with greater sadness:

I have lived long enough. My way of life
Is fall'n into the sear, the yellow leaf,
That that which should accompany old age,
As honor, love, obedience, troops of friends,
I must not look to have; but, in their stead,
Curses not loud but deep, mouth-honor,
    breath,
Which the poor heart would fain deny, and
    dare not.

To say that no one who has become a bloody tyrant would speak in this way is pointless; he would *feel* in this way, or so we are convinced.

By feeling the pangs that we would feel if we were in his place, and by passing our judgments upon himself, Macbeth attaches us to him and consequently himself to us. We cannot view him with cold objectivity as something strange and apart. The unnaturalness of his acts is always counterpoised by the naturalness of his actions: his hesitant overtures to Banquo, his volubility after Duncan's death, his dazed petulance at the appearance of the ghost:

The time has been
That, when the brains were out, the man
    would die,
And there an end; but now they rise again,
With twenty mortal murders on their crowns,
And push us from our stools.

There is something here both grimly humorous and affecting, this killer's speaking in the accents of a hurt child. We should not ascribe Macbeth's humanity to the automatic working of Shakespeare's sympathetic nature. There is nothing casual about it. If Macbeth were other than he is, less like ourselves, he would be a less powerful symbol of our own worst potentialities and the abyss we have escaped. There is nothing of him in Cornwall or Iago for all of Shakespeare's sympathetic nature.

It is hard to believe that so universal a work was calculated to the meridian of any particular person, but there are arguments favoring the possibility. James Stuart, who had ascended the English throne and become the nominal patron of Shakespeare's company a few years before *Macbeth* was written, was supposedly descended from Banquo and was intensely interested in witchcraft; moreover he had assumed in 1605 the prerogative of curing the "king's evil" instituted by Edward the Confessor and mentioned somewhat irrelevantly in the play. On the other hand, one may argue that had Shakespeare's primary concern been to please the monarch, he might have dramatized more creditable episodes in Scottish history, might have drawn a more flattering portrait of Banquo, and might have seized the opportunity to eulogize the eighth figure in the show of kings (Act IV, Scene 1) since this figure represents James himself.

From "Introduction" (retitled "Thou Shalt Not Kill") by Alfred Harbage from *The Tragedy of Macbeth* by William Shakespeare, edited by Alfred Harbage. Copyright © 1956 by *Penguin Books USA Inc.* Reprinted by permission of the publisher.

# Doers of Deeds

*by* **Michael Long**

## Bloody Execution

Shakespeare often begins a tragedy with somebody's description of the protagonist before he comes onstage. We hear of Marcius as "chief enemy to the people" before he bursts in full of fury. We hear of the "good and gracious" Timon before he sweeps on distributing largess. We hear of Antony falling into "dotage," and then the great lover strolls on in leisured magnificence. We hear whispers of Lear's odd shifts of favor, and then he comes on in state to express his "darker purpose." And we are told that Othello is a vainglorious soldier full of "bombast circumstance," as well as a lascivious, black lover who has stolen a white woman, before the man himself appears as if to answer these nasty charges. The simple technique creates expectation. It also tells an audience whom to watch, and why.

Macbeth's introduction comes from the wounded captain in Act I, Scene 2. The captain is a fine, epic soldier with a bent for vivid rhetoric, and the picture he paints is memorable. He evokes the rebel Macdonwald with the "multiplying villainies of nature" swarming on him like flies on a carcass surrounded by an equally swarming horde of "kerns and gallowglasses" drummed up for his cause in the Western Isles, and then he describes the tremendous irruption of Macbeth into these swirls of movement, cutting his way to the center of things to dominate them with his deeds and his presence:

> . . . Brave Macbeth—well he deserves that
> name—
> Disdaining Fortune, with his brandished steel,
> Which smoked with bloody execution,
> Like valor's minion carved out his passage
> Till he faced the slave;
> Which nev'r shook hands, nor bade farewell
> to him,
> Till he unseamed him from the nave to th'
> chops,
> And fixed his head upon our battlements.
> —Act 1, Scene 2, lines 16–23

This "bloody execution" sounds brutal; but the epic rhetoric also makes it sound magnificent.

The Macbeth we later meet does not disappoint the expectations raised by this dramatic opening account of him. He is brutal, but he has his epic magnificence too, and one of his chief roles is to be the sort of decisive doer, intervener, or irruptive agent whom the captain describes. The captain makes us think about violent action, but also about action in itself, as he pictures Macbeth's terrible, thrilling intervention into things and his ruthless domination of the field. This will be a play about a man who does and about the momentous deed that he does. It will be a play about doing and about that spectacular, frightening spirit of "bloody execution."

Macbeth cannot lie passive like Duncan "shut up in measureless content," nor stand like Banquo "in the great hand of God," waiting patiently for the unraveling of destiny. They may live in tranquillity at the slow pace of unfolding events, as the martlets do, suspended in their airy bed where "the heaven's breath / Smells wooingly," but the restless Macbeth must be up and doing. Early on he hopes that chance may crown him "without my stir," but he soon realizes that it will not. He must stir, and act, and thus confront the fatality of individual deeds.

Shakespeare makes this sense of the existential fatality of action resonate powerfully in the play, and his principal method for doing so is extraordinarily simple. *Macbeth* activates every possible resonance of the verb *to do. Do, did, done,* and the cognate noun *deed* are words stirred into vivid life by an imagination dwelling profoundly on the fatal business of "blood execution" or, indeed, any kind of execution. They carry the play's cogent exploration of what it is to be a separate, acting individual rather than an unperturbed particle of social acquiescence or of the breath of nature's quiet.

They are aided in this by another word, almost as simple, and allied both conceptually and onomatopoeically with *do* and *deed*. This is the verb *to dare,* upon which the play also dwells to wonderful effect. Macbeth does. Macbeth dares to do. These simple words are made to yield every gram of their poetic and philosophical potential.

## Act I: "If It Were Done When 'Tis Done"

In Act I, Scene 3, Macbeth entertains his hope that things might happen "without my stir." But in the next scene, Duncan names Malcolm as his heir, Macbeth's fond hopes die, and his imagination turns to the mechanisms whereby desires become deeds. He will have to stir, to "o'erleap" the obstacle in his path, and he will have to act, hidden guiltily from the lights of the natural world:

*Drama Study Guide:* **The Tragedy of Macbeth**

HRW MATERIAL COPYRIGHTED UNDER NOTICE APPEARING EARLIER IN THIS WORK.

**13**

Stars, hide your fires;
Let not light see my black and deep desires. . . .
—Act I, Scene 4, lines 50–51

Banquo and the king stand before him talking pleasurably and easefully. They are still in the old, quiet world, but Macbeth has moved to another realm. This is the start of his career as an existential agent and the start of the formidable poetic career of the verb *to do:*

. . . Let that be
Which the eye fears, when it is done, to see.
—Act I, Scene 4, lines 52–53

In the next scene, when his wife receives his letter and the witches' poison starts to course through her veins, the key words sound again in juggling conjuration:

Thou'dst have, great Glamis,
That which cries, "Thus thou must do" if thou
have it;
And that which rather thou dost fear to do
Than wishest should be undone.
—Act I, Scene 5, lines 21–24

Lady Macbeth conceives of herself as a natural doer, made for "business" and "dispatch," but we shall see how the stresses of the interventionist role will be too much for her. Macbeth's greater trepidation is well placed. It is more appropriate to the terrors attendant upon the business of doing and to the explosive powers that lie within these fascinating words.

In the last scene of Act I, the key words come thick and fast. Macbeth wrestles with his fears and desires, and the key words flicker hypnotically before his captivated eyes:

If it were done when 'tis done, then 'twere well
It were done quickly.
—Act I, Scene 7, lines 1–2

They draw him on with the idea of decisive, "be-all" and "end-all" action. Then comes a counter-movement, equally strong, where he remembers the great taboos that speak "against the deed" and shrinks in anticipation of the outrage that will be felt when "the horrid deed" is revealed.

Then his wife chides him for his doubter's sense of "I dare not," and he seizes on that word too and squeezes it tightly:

I dare do all that may become a man;
Who dares do more is none.
—Act I, Scene 7, lines 46–47

The word *man* has joined the wrestling knot of words, and Lady Macbeth keeps it there to shame him into action:

When you durst do it, then you were a man. . . .
—Act I, Scene 7, line 49

By the end of the scene, Macbeth is resolved, and a dark, subdued hymn to doing sounds beneath the couple's dialogue. Lady Macbeth talks horribly of an outrageous license to do what one will:

What cannot you and I perform upon
Th' unguarded Duncan . . . ?
—Act I, Scene 7, lines 69–70

Macbeth hits on the clever idea of incriminating the grooms so that people will think "they have don't," and Lady Macbeth chimes excitedly back that there will be none "who dares receive it other." They chant together, work up their courage, and bring Macbeth to readiness for "this terrible feat."

## Act II: "I Have Done the Deed"

As Act II opens, the incantations stop while Banquo evokes the magically profound "pleasure" and "content" of Duncan's soul, but after this beautiful linguistic interlude the phantom dagger appears. It lures on the "heat-oppressèd brain" of Macbeth, rekindles "the heat of deeds," and renews the fatal drive to action: "I go, and it is done. . . ."

In Act II, Scene 2, the awesome words are whispered in terror in the dark. Lady Macbeth fears the attempt has been bungled ("'tis not done!") and dwells on the awful irony whereby they might be confounded not by doing "the deed" but by failing to do it. She too is now more alert to the scale of what is involved, increasing the weight on the key verb by using it in another momentous context:

Had he not resembled
My father as he slept, I had done't.
—Act II, Scene 2, lines 12–13

By the time the crime is accomplished, the collocation of verb and noun is enough to sound the depths of irrevocability: "I have done the deed."

The now appalling noun *deed(s)* shudders in their minds three more times in the scene ("these deeds," "this deed," "my deed"); and in the midst of them, Macbeth finds another memorable collocation, linking doing with daring in an expression of the utmost horror:

I am afraid to think what I have done;
Look on't again I dare not.
—Act II, Scene 2, lines 51–52

Such simple words will never be simple again.

After this great scene, Shakespeare lets the words go for a while before bringing them back to close the act. In Act II, Scene 4, with the Old Man's

*Drama Study Guide: The Tragedy of Macbeth*

talk of "the deed that's done," Ross's reference to "this more than bloody deed," and Macduff's mention simply of "the deed," we hear uneasy speakers probe the key words suspiciously. They keep what has happened at arm's length by referring to it darkly as "the deed," as if they wanted to keep their eyes averted from some abomination or their persons out of striking distance of it.

The atmosphere of their talk makes Macbeth's deed of destruction seem like the deed of Adam and Eve. All nature has fallen into darkness and savagery as a result of it. Macduff already knows that Ross will not see things "well done" at Macbeth's coronation. From such catastrophe, recovery cannot be so quick, for Macbeth has made "a breach in nature" with his tremendous intervention into the settled state of things, and these three are now living amidst the "ruin" that, as in Eden, gained its "wasteful entrance" when that breach was made.

## Act III: "A Deed of Dreadful Note"

But deeds lead to deeds, and in Act III the words return, with the Second Murderer "reckless what / I do" and Macbeth determined that his new deed, the killing of Banquo, "must be done tonight." In Act III, Scene 2, Lady Macbeth tries to kill the words off with the finality of her statement that "what's done is done," but it will be a long time yet before the terrible energy of these words has run down. Macbeth, better apprised than his wife of the enormity of what they have unloosed, promises to keep up with the race of things:

> . . . There shall be done
> A deed of dreadful note
> —Act III, Scene 2, lines 43–44

while his bewildered wife asks him, "What's to be done?"; but he, as if sensing her inability to stay the course on which they are now set, decides to keep his doings to himself:

> Be innocent of the knowledge, dearest chuck,
> Till thou applaud the deed.
> —Act III, Scene 2, lines 45–46

There is now a hardening in Macbeth. The fateful words no longer frighten him so much. He begins to use them with perceptible relish, sensing their menace and less awed than he was. That "dearest chuck" is gross and sinister in a way that is new; and also new are tellingly banal uses of the key words in the next two scenes. In Act III, Scene 3, the murderers banalize the words with shoptalk about "what we have to do" and the report they will deliver on "how much is done," and in Act III, Scene 4, there is a thuggery in their professional talk of cutting throats ("That I did for him"). Mac-

beth seems to catch this thuggish note from them like a contagion, hoping that they not only cut Banquo's throat but also "did the like for Fleance" and calling one of them a "nonpareil" among men "if thou didst it." At some level he seems to be enjoying this new brashness, as if it were a man's talk for which his "dearest chuck" is unfit.

But he loses his swagger when the ghost appears to shake his "gory lock" at him. The key words are now used to cry helplessly "Which of you have done this?" and to disavow the role of agent altogether: "Thou can'st not say I did it." To fight back this terror, he will need the talismanic verb *to dare*. He will need to claim that he

> . . . dare look on that
> Which might appall the devil
> —Act III, Scene 4, lines 59–60

and to face down the charge of cowardice with cries of "What man dare, I dare" and "dare me to the desert." These are cries that come swirling out of a mind in panic, until at last he regains some shreds of composure, enabling him to return to things that "must be acted" and to the accent of menace: "We are yet but young in deed."

## Act IV: "A Deed Without a Name"

To make himself less "young in deed" in Act IV, he returns to the witches, who were the original inspiration for the impulse to do. As he sets foot in their den, he cries out with the verb: "What is't you do?" and they chant back the noun as if in ritual response: "A deed without a name."

While Duncan's court lived at the pace of acquiescence and unassertiveness, this den is the holy place of a religion of deeds. It is where Macbeth goes for inspiration when his heart "throbs to know" and when, unable to wait upon the quiet rhythms of nature's evolutions, he is prepared to see

> . . . the treasure
> Of nature's germens tumble all together,
> Even till destruction sicken
> —Act IV, Scene 1, lines 58–60

to satisfy his restless desire. He gets his inspiration. He emerges from the ordeal nerved again, resolved to kill for a third time and with the key words on his lips:

> The flighty purpose never is o'ertook
> Unless the deed go with it.
> —Act IV, Scene 1, lines 145–146
> And even now,
> To crown my thoughts with acts, be it thought
>    and done. . . .
> —Act IV, Scene 1, lines 148–149

*Drama Study Guide: The Tragedy of Macbeth*

No boasting like a fool;
This deed I'll do. . . .
—Act IV, Scene 1, lines 153–154

## Act V: "Little Is to Do"

The deed he does is the killing of Macduff's wife and children, and after it Shakespeare leaves the idea of doing alone, as if, after such an outrage, it could now have no further moral or poetic content. The remainder of Macbeth's life is led in Act V within the fortress of Dunsinane, where, incapable of any more doing, he paces out the long, halting soliloquy of his despair, interspersed with outbursts of rage against puny people like servants, unwilling followers, a messenger, and "the boy Malcolm." It is the nadir of the great doer, hemmed in and frustrated in every desire.

Here, as his way of life falls into the sere, there is no further activation of *do* and *deed,* and the idea of daring takes on a desperate, last-ditch quality. He is tied to the stage, with only growls of defiance as evidence of his former courage and nerve. We have seen enough of deeds and doers. Doing has turned out merely to be butchery, and the compelling rhythms of the key words have run down.

As the rhythms of doing fade, a different rhythm, not felt since Duncan was alive, brings time round in its cycle again to make the autumnal Macbeth "ripe for shaking." His fall does not feel like an act performed by men, attributable to human agency. It happens when the time is ripe, in accordance with some internal logic in events that is not subject to will and intervention. We wait until the long night of his deed-filled tyranny at last "finds the day," and then we find the fortified castle being "gently rend'red" to beautifully unurgent men.

In harmony with the ease and gentleness of that phrase come two magnificent usages of the key words that help slow the play to a less cruel pace. The first comes from Macduff, who has no quarrel with anybody except Macbeth and who, rather than fight against men innocently embroiled in the tyrant's career, would prefer to leave his sword "undeeded." The second comes from Old Siward, inviting Malcolm simply to walk into the castle of Dunsinane, crossing its threshold effortlessly since, miraculously, "little is to do." The tenor of these phrases is relievingly unassertive, as if what were occurring involved no more than acquiescence in the eternal cycles of things.

The human world comes back into contact with an inner, preconscious rhythm. Green branches bring the forest's silence and fertility back into human society, and the young king promises that "what's more to do" will, as if in response to the forest's presence, be "planted newly with the time." Things will be done according to the old, quiet rhythm of things, "in measure, time, and place," with no doing, daring, "bloody execution," or "dispatch" disrupting the free-flowing "grace of Grace." We have not heard such sustained sounds of leisure and peace since Duncan was alive or since Macbeth started to conjure the turbulent life out of dangerous words or since the witches wound up the infernal plot with that frantic cry that has proved to be so laden with import:

I'll do, I'll do, and I'll do.
—Act I, Scene 3, line 10

"Doers of Deeds" from *Twayne's New Critical Introduction to Shakespeare: Macbeth* by Michael Long. Copyright © 1989 by Michael Long. Reprinted by permission of *Harvester Wheatsheaf, a division of Simon & Schuster, Inc.*

# Elements of the Play

## Key Literary Elements of the Play

**Protagonist:**  Macbeth

**Antagonist:**  Scottish nobles, greed, ambition

**Conflicts:**  person versus self, person versus person

**Significant Techniques:**  foreshadowing, characterization, mood, conflict, resolution, theme, climax, figurative language, dramatic irony, paradox, blank verse, suspense, symbolism, turning point, soliloquy, dumb show, tragedy

**Setting:**  Scotland and England in the eleventh century

## Cast of Characters in the Play

### Main Characters

**DUNCAN,** king of Scotland and a mild-mannered ruler. Duncan is murdered by Macbeth.

**MALCOLM,** a son of Duncan. When Duncan is murdered, Malcolm, fearful of meeting the same fate, flees to England. There, Macduff beseeches him to come back to Scotland and claim his rightful throne. When an army of Englishmen and rebel Scots defeats and kills Macbeth, Malcolm becomes king of Scotland.

**MACBETH,** general of the king's army, afterward king of Scotland. Macbeth is a complex character: Imaginative and sensitive, he at first recoils from the idea of murdering Duncan even though he wishes to become king. At the prodding of his wife, he does the deed; then, after he wears the crown, he begins to understand that crime begets crime. Fearful on his shaky throne, he commits murder after murder until the Scottish thanes revolt and depose him. The influence of the weird sisters on Macbeth is problematic; probably to Shakespeare they represented objectified witches, but the title *weird* ties them to the old Anglo-Saxon conception of a person's *wyrd,* or fate.

**BANQUO,** general of the king's army. Banquo acts as a foil for Macbeth. The witches predict that Banquo's issue will be kings, but Banquo does nothing to hasten the day. He is murdered by Macbeth because Macbeth realizes that Banquo suspects him of the murder of Duncan and because the witches have predicted that Banquo's issue, rather than Macbeth's, will rule Scotland.

**MACDUFF,** Macbeth's special nemesis. Macduff circumvents the prophecy made to Macbeth by the witches.

**LADY MACBETH,** wife of Macbeth. She has often been played as villain par excellence. Certainly she seems more resolute and bloodthirsty than her husband in the early stages of the play. All her ambition seems to be for Macbeth, however, rather than for herself; she steels him to do what he really wants to do. Further, her sleepwalking scene, in Act V, shows that she possesses a conscience. Shakespeare does not show Lady Macbeth as her husband's partner in crime after the murder of Duncan, and she does not even appear in Act IV when Macbeth is undergoing his greatest degeneration.

### Supporting Characters

**ANGUS,** Scottish noble.

**CAITHNESS,** Scottish noble.

**DONALBAIN,** young son of Duncan.

**FLEANCE,** Banquo's son, who manages to escape his father's fate.

**HECATE,** the queen of the witches.

**LENNOX,** Scottish noble.

**LADY MACDUFF,** killed by order of Macbeth.

**MENTEITH,** Scottish noble.

**ROSS,** Scottish noble.

SEYTON, an officer attending Macbeth.

SIWARD, Earl of Northumberland.

YOUNG SIWARD, son of Northumberland.

THREE WITCHES, the weird sisters.

Also a GENTLEWOMAN; an OLD MAN, an ENGLISH DOCTOR, and a SCOTTISH DOCTOR; a CAPTAIN; a PORTER; a BOY, a son of Macduff; APPARITIONS, LORDS, OFFICERS, SOLDIERS, MURDERERS, ATTENDANTS, and MESSENGERS.

## The Themes of the Play

*Macbeth,* as everyone knows, is a tragedy, a kind of play in which human actions have their inevitable consequences, in which the characters' bad deeds, errors, mistakes, and crimes are never forgiven or rectified. The characters in a comedy do not live under this iron law of cause and effect; they can do whatever they please so long as they amuse their audience, and at the end of the play the funny mess they have made is easily cleaned up. But in tragedy an ill-judged action will remorselessly lead to catastrophe, usually but not necessarily a death or multiple deaths. In *Macbeth* a brave and intelligent man deliberately murders one of his fellow men—his friend, his kinsman, his guest, his king—and then he must immediately, as a consequence of his first murder, kill two other innocent men. After that he cannot turn back from his evil course: It leads him to further appalling crimes and finally to disgrace, alienation, isolation, despair, violent death, and decapitation.

As students read *Macbeth,* encourage them to think about this depiction of the consequences of one man's evil deed and to decide how the following themes are part of Shakespeare's concern:

1. Violence and bloodshed result when the prescribed social order is tampered with.
2. The qualities of good and evil, strength and weakness, are often combined in a single individual.
3. Brave, honest, and noble persons can be seduced by power and ambition, and so turned into tyrants.
4. Internal desires and fears can be more influential than exterior reality.

## A Tragic Hero

*Macbeth* belongs to the type of tragedy that is perhaps the best known, for it is the one to which the great majority of the most famous tragic plays and stories belong. It is the type of tragedy that Aristotle wrote about in his *Poetics,* the earliest and still the most celebrated and the most concise treatise on the theory of tragedy.

This type of tragedy focuses most sharply on the ambiguity in the character of the tragic hero. Aristotle defines this hero as "a man who is neither outstanding in virtue and righteousness, nor is it through wickedness that he falls into misfortune, but through some flaw." The two terms Aristotle uses to describe this tragic flaw are *hubris* and *hamartia.* The first term is usually translated as "pride," which is an excess of will—a *character* defect. The second, *hamartia,* is usually rendered as "error in judgment," a deficiency in knowledge—an *intellectual* defect. Generally speaking, both these aspects of the tragic flaw—an excess of will and a deficiency in knowledge—are present in Macbeth. Besides being willfully self-assertive,

Macbeth also fails to anticipate the full consequences of his actions. He makes a fatal miscalculation about reality.

*Macbeth* is the story of the fall of a great soldier, a nobleman whose qualities as a leader put him in a place so close to the throne of Scotland that he is tempted to take that throne away from its rightful occupant, King Duncan. In doing so, however, Macbeth is forced to violate one of the most fundamental laws of man and God: "Thou shalt not kill." Moreover, since he is a man with a keen sense of the value of human institutions and the importance of order in human society, he violates the law of his own nature. The consequences of his tragic act are sure, swift, and inevitable. They involve him and his nation in a series of disasters that gradually narrow the range of his free choice, tear him and his country to pieces, isolate him from his fellow men, and lead to his death. Only with his death is the order that he disrupted reestablished and the equilibrium in nature and society restored.

*Drama Study Guide: **The Tragedy of Macbeth***

# The Brevity of the Play

One curious and striking thing about *The Tragedy of Macbeth* is that it is so brief. With only 2,100 lines, it is one of the shortest of all Shakespeare's plays and definitely the shortest of the tragedies: *Hamlet, Othello,* and *King Lear* are almost half again as long. This brevity is the key to *Macbeth*'s uniqueness. Shakespeare's comedies are sometimes brief, but his tragedies and histories are complex, with many characters and several secondary plots. *Hamlet,* for example, is heavily peopled, almost crowded; it has no center, and its hero is surrounded by baffling complications. *King Lear,* too, is purposely gigantic, so as to overwhelm its audience. But *Macbeth* is swift and single-minded. There are few subplots and very little comic mix. So intent is its single sweeping effect that it limits Lady Macbeth's role in the plot and abandons Donalbain in the second half. The play moves at a compact, powerful, fierce pace—just as Macbeth moves inexorably in his path toward utter ruin.

# Visual Aspects of the Play

Here is a brief discussion of some of the features that help make *Macbeth* so easy for readers to visualize. The ideas presented here, and others, can be found in *Twayne's New Critical Introductions to Shakespeare: Macbeth* by Michael Long (Twayne Publishers, 1989).

## Castles and Chambers

In a play as brief and as tightly woven as *Macbeth,* location and terrain are never accidental. The three human dwellings in the play contrast powerfully with one another and with the wilderness around them.

The first important domestic setting is Macbeth's own home at Inverness—with its deceptive atmosphere of warm hospitality and happy family life. Food and lodging are provided, and it is, until terror takes hold, a "pleasant seat" where martlets breed and Duncan feels himself to be a welcome guest.

After the murder and the seizure of power, the setting changes to the palace at Forres. This is a royal palace, bigger, grander, and more formal than the Inverness dwelling. It is here that Macbeth attempts to live out his doomed kingship.

When the mask finally collapses and Macbeth is ruling by power alone, the setting moves to the castle of Dunsinane. Macbeth tries to secure the castle for himself—"Great Dunsinane he strongly fortifies. / Some say he's mad; others, that lesser hate him, / Do call it valiant fury . . ." (Act V, Scene 2, lines 12–14)—but it becomes the bleak setting for his final solitude.

Inverness, Forres, and Dunsinane are the important settings of the play, but there are also important locales that are never visited. These are two bedchambers unseen by the audience but unfor-gettably evoked in verse. In both, terrible disruptions occur—disruptions that shatter sleep and all that sleep can stand for.

In one bedchamber sleeps Duncan on his fatal visit to Inverness. So vivid are the images—the bed, the blood on the sheets, the old man, and the blood all over "his silver skin"—that we have to stop and remind ourselves that we never enter this room. Two recollections by Lady Macbeth imprint the scene on our minds: "Had he not resembled / My father as he slept, I had don't" (Act II, Scene 2, lines 12–13) and, after the murder, "Yet who would have thought the old man to have had so much blood in him?" (Act V, Scene 1, lines 38–39).

The second bedchamber is that of Lady Macbeth herself. The doctor and an attendant of Lady Macbeth's talk about it at the beginning of Act V. In that room, Lady Macbeth lives in tormented fear of the dark.

Dreadful violence is done in Duncan's chamber, dreadful violence is suffered by the mind in Lady Macbeth's.

## Three Props

Props, or movable articles used to embellish and comment on a setting (the word is a shortening of *properties*), have a unique role in the play. *Macbeth* contains three of Shakespeare's greatest props. The first is the feasting table in Act III, Scene 4. It speaks of hospitality, ceremonial order and degree, the security of a well-organized indoor world in contrast to the darkness and the danger outside. The Scottish lord comments on this prop in Act III, Scene 6: "We may again / give to our tables meat . . ." (lines 33–34).

The second prop—the caldron of Act IV, Scene 1—is far different. Music ushers guests to the feasting table, but chanting and incantations introduce the horrible caldron. In it nature is torn to fragments. Bits and scraps are tumbled together in "gruel thick and slab"—the antithesis of the food of feasts and banquets.

The third great prop is Birnam Wood, with its symbolism of returning spring. New life is evoked by the advance of the forest's "leavy screens," so different from the military maneuvers of the history plays and the metal and leather armor of *Julius Caesar*.

## Four Apparitions

*Macbeth* is unique in its reliance on apparitions. The witches, who appear as beings unknown and unnamed, swirl out of the mist at the beginning of the play and then vanish. Only *A Midsummer Night's Dream* and *The Tempest* give so large a role to supernatural beings.

Another apparition is the airborne dagger, which may be real ("sensible / To feeling") or "a dagger of the mind." Like the witches, this apparition lives on the boundary between the real and the imagined.

The ghost of Banquo lives on this same boundary—visible to Macbeth but invisible to others. Like the ghost of Hamlet's father on his second appearance (when only Hamlet can see him), the ghost of Banquo utters truths with his silent presence.

The final apparitions are conjured up from the caldron. They, too, are both real and unreal, and they drive Macbeth to distraction.

*Drama Study Guide: **The Tragedy of Macbeth***

# Teaching the Play

## Objectives

1. To analyze Shakespeare's use of blank verse
2. To understand Shakespeare's use of foreshadowing to build suspense
3. To identify methods of characterization
4. To analyze mood
5. To identify conflict and resolution
6. To identify themes
7. To identify climax
8. To write an interpretation of character, a character analysis, a parody
9. To analyze imagery and figurative language

## Introducing the Play

### The Renaissance Theater

Review with your students the material about the Renaissance theater (pages 1–7) in the HRW Classics edition of *Macbeth*. From it students should get a feel for an aspect of Shakespearean theater that they may not have considered before: the physical production of each play. The need to make a play manageable on a stage is often overlooked in a study of the play as a great work of literature. In addition, students may be surprised to learn how much of our knowledge about the Globe is based on surmise and deduction rather than factual accounts.

With your students, discuss the following important points.

- Medieval drama originated in church ceremonies.
- Before the Renaissance the following types of plays were produced: **miracle/mystery, morality,** and **interlude.**
- The first public theater was built in the late sixteenth century.
- The Globe, owned by Shakespeare's theater company, is the most famous public theater.
- Renaissance theater sets were meager.
- Renaissance theaters were ornate.
- Many Renaissance plays included processions.
- Music, especially songs, was an important part of Renaissance play performances.
- Acting companies also performed in castles and manor houses.

### The Five-Part Dramatic Structure

Also discuss the five-part dramatic structure of Shakespearean drama, which generally (although not absolutely) corresponds to a play's five acts. You may want to duplicate for your students the following diagram and definitions.

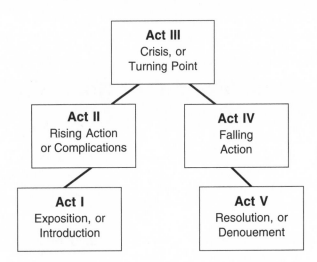

The **exposition** or the **introduction** establishes tone, setting, some of the main characters, previous events necessary for understanding the play's action, and the main **conflict,** or problem.

The **rising action** is a series of **complications** besetting the protagonist that arise when the protagonist takes action to resolve his or her main conflict.

*Drama Study Guide: The Tragedy of Macbeth*

HRW MATERIAL COPYRIGHTED UNDER NOTICE APPEARING EARLIER IN THIS WORK.

21

The **crisis,** or **turning point,** is the moment of choice for the protagonist, the moment when the forces of conflict come together and the situation will either improve or inexorably deteriorate. The crisis usually occurs in Act III.

The **falling action** presents the incidents resulting from the protagonist's decision at the turning point. In tragedy these incidents necessarily emphasize the play's destructive forces but often include an episode of possible salvation, as well as comic scenes. These are the playwright's means of maintaining suspense and relieving the tension as the catastrophe approaches.

The **resolution,** or **denouement,** is the conclusion of the play, the unraveling of the plot, which in tragedy includes the **catastrophe** of the hero's and others' deaths. The **climax,** or emotional peak, usually occurs right before the denouement.

## A Preface to *Macbeth*

In teaching *Macbeth,* you must be guided by the time you have to spend on the play and by the ability levels of your students. Still, if at all possible, two important instructional strategies should be implemented.

First, students should hear *Macbeth* read by an actor or see it performed onstage or on film. Several good sound recordings are available, as are video recordings. Students who hear *Macbeth* read aloud will be aided by the actors' speech intona-

tions and so will likely better understand the plot.

Second, students should be introduced to Aristotle's definition of tragedy and the seven characteristics of tragedy. Undoubtedly they will understand the play better if they consider whether it fits Aristotle's definition and follows the guidelines for tragedy. They should also consider the nature of the tragic hero and the tragic flaw, for in the characterization lie the cause and effect of the action.

Plan to discuss Aristotle's definition of tragedy before students begin reading *Macbeth.* Have them consider this quotation:

> Tragedy is an imitation of some action that is important, entire, and of a proper magnitude, by language embellished and rendered pleasurable, but by different means in different parts, in the way not of narration, but of action, effecting through pity and terror the refinement of such passions.

Point out that tragedy is an imitation of an action important enough to cause a series of related actions to occur. The playwright, through actors, will use language to convey the action. The playwright will emphasize the action itself and not a simple telling of the action. Finally, the playwright will provide pity and terror in characterization and in the cause-and-effect relationship of the tragic hero. This last aspect is very important because with it the playwright can bring about a catharsis, or a purging.

# Reading and Performing the Play

Some teachers like to plunge their students immediately into a brief "performance" of the play. If you want to try this, assign parts for an informal performance of Act I, Scene 1. In this scene, which typifies Shakespeare's interest in the supernatural, we are introduced to Macbeth by other characters in the play.

Don't have a rehearsal; just get three students up in front of the class, books in hand, and have them read their parts. Unless your class is especially small, you can probably have several groups take turns performing the scene. You'll undoubtedly be surprised at how quickly the students will catch on to the mood of the scene. With a few of these impromptu performances, some of the hurdles to the language will have been cleared.

When you assign the reading of Act I, go over the format of the text carefully. Show students that

unfamiliar words, phrases, and allusions are marked with a symbol and explained in a footnote that is keyed to the appropriate line number. Next, read a few of the Guided Reading questions, which begin on page 38 of this guide. Explain that these questions aid understanding by pointing to details of the plot and eliciting interpretations of character, language, and staging.

Use the first class period after students' have read the act to allow them to *hear* Shakespeare's language. Read the opening scene yourself, play a sound recording, or show a film. Doing so will provide a model of correct phrasing and will show how much an actor's interpretation adds to the play's meaning.

A resource that is full of good ideas about teaching the play by means of performance is the Folger Library's *Shakespeare Set Free,* edited by

*Drama Study Guide: **The Tragedy of Macbeth***

Peggy O'Brien (Washington Square Press, published by Pocket Books).

## Understanding the Literary Elements

Remind students of the genre they are studying: Drama is a literary *and a* performing art. *Macbeth,* though written to be acted, is splendid reading. As you read, play recordings, and show films, students should see how gestures, timing, staging, sound effects, and actors' interpretations can affect meaning. Although the words do not change from performance to performance, the audience's perceptions and reactions do. The questions and exercises in this Study Guide will help students appreciate Shakespeare's mastery of dramatic structure and literary techniques. By reading and studying this play, students should come to see how Shakespeare keeps the audience's interest.

## Strategies for Reading the Play

Refer students to the objectives that are listed at the beginning of this section. Their reading of these objectives should help them establish a purpose in reading *Macbeth.* Also help them monitor their own reading by asking able readers to take turns reading parts. As one student reads aloud, ask others to determine the possible motivations of the characters being depicted.

It is important to focus students on understanding *Macbeth* in terms of tragedy. As they read the play, refer them to Aristotle's definition and what the philosopher said we expect of tragedy. In doing so, you will be helping students understand the characterizations of Macbeth and Lady Macbeth. You may even ask students to determine whether they think either or both main characters are tragic in Aristotle's sense.

In addition, you may ask students to write their own summaries of each scene in *Macbeth;* if they do, ask them to express their views of the tragedy. For example, they might describe their perceptions of the importance of fate and free choice as implied in a particular scene. They might discuss the changes in the characters of Macbeth and Lady Macbeth. They might consider the cause-and-effect relationship depicted in the tragedy.

Another important strategy is to have students place Shakespeare's work on a time line. As they do this, they will come to understand Shakespeare's place in British history and literature in terms of other important writers. From a time line, students may better understand that the language of Shakespeare is not the same as that of Chaucer, nor is it the same as that of Milton. If students have read selections from *The Canterbury Tales* and have looked at the Prologue in Middle English,

they will understand that the language of the Renaissance is much more similar to Modern English than is Chaucer's language. Nor is Shakespeare's language as difficult to understand as Milton's, with its often inverted sentence structure.

As they read, have students take note of Shakespeare's imagery and his reliance on figures of speech. Remind students that Shakespearean drama is precisely that—drama—but Shakespeare was a poet at heart, and as a consequence, much of the language of his plays is highly poetic.

Before the class embarks on the first act, review the meaning of the terms *metaphor, simile,* and *personification,* asking volunteers to provide examples of each.

As was mentioned earlier, if it is possible to obtain a professional recording, you might wish to provide students with an oral interpretation of selected scenes. Otherwise, you are advised to read portions aloud yourself. Devote a part of each class period to the oral presentation of several scenes, and assign the balance of the act for homework. Use the beginning of the following period to cover the Making Meanings questions and to address any issues or problems students raise. The final series of questions and the writing assignments, which are voluminous, will require another class period. You might also plan on setting aside additional time for the essays that accompany the text of the play, if it is your intention to use them.

For your convenience, scene-by-scene plot summaries have been provided for each of the five acts.

## Establishing a Procedure

Before you begin to teach the play, examine the teaching resources in this Study Guide; they provide a wealth of ideas for classroom work, homework assignments, projects, reports, and tests. If possible, obtain a film of *Macbeth,* as well as books and audiovisual materials about Shakespeare, his times, and the Globe Theater. (Check with your school or public library for the availability of a television production or film of the play.) Then, determine which projects and writing exercises you will assign, decide how you will present each act, and prepare a daily reading and assignment schedule.

Use the first two or three days to prepare students for the reading. Discuss the Introduction (pages 1–18 of the HRW Classics edition of *Macbeth*), and enhance the historical information with filmstrips, films, or illustrated books. Do not let students be intimidated by the poetry of the play; introduce terms and read passages aloud, but delay scrutiny of the dramatic technique until they are interested in the play and more comfortable

*Drama Study Guide: The Tragedy of Macbeth*

HRW MATERIAL COPYRIGHTED UNDER NOTICE APPEARING EARLIER IN THIS WORK.

23

with its language. In the same way, briefly introduce the five-part structure of Shakespearean drama. In doing this, you will be providing students with a vocabulary for discussing form, which they will do with much more understanding as they follow the plot.

Finally, distribute your schedule for studying the play, and explain long-range projects and writing exercises. For example, if you want the class to undertake small-group activities, you should assign students to groups as this point so that they can begin working together.

Here is a procedure for presenting each act of the play. Before students begin reading, establish the time and place of each scene (if you desire, summarize the plot or distribute a plot summary); assign vocabulary words, discussion questions, and any writing exercises; designate passages for oral reading; alert students to any scenes for which you will play a recording; and remind students of quizzes and scheduled project reports.

Schedule at least two days of class time for each act. Vary activities from act to act as much as possible. The suggested combination of oral readings, discussion, viewings of scenes, and project reports should keep students stimulated throughout the course of the play.

After students finish reading the play, show a filmed production straight through; students will know the play very well by then, and the viewing will synthesize their experience of its elements.

## Providing for Different Levels of Ability

Work individually with students who have particular difficulty with Shakespeare's language, and emphasize paraphrasing in both written and oral work. To prepare students with limited English, have them make full use of plot summaries, vocabulary definitions, and audiovisual aids in conjunction with small-group projects and writing exercises.

Additional options for teaching the play are described, act by act, beginning on this page.

# Options for Teaching the Play

Use these ideas to modify your instruction to suit the needs of individual students.

# Act I

## Strategies for Inclusion

**SPECIAL NEEDS** Because of drama's dependence on visualization and the very strong visual element in Shakespeare's poetry, pay special attention to **imagery** in *Macbeth,* for which students with visual impairment will need explanations. For example, in Act I, Scene 5, lines 64–65, students need to know that the foliage of the flower conceals the snake—the scene looks innocent and inviting, and the poison is hidden. Without explanation, students may not realize how this statement continues the **theme** of appearance versus reality.

**ENGLISH LANGUAGE DEVELOPMENT** Before students read, discuss the meaning of the word *temptation.* Prompt discussion with questions such as these: What things tempt people to act in a way that is wrong or contrary to their natures? In such cases, is the result usually good or bad? After they have read Act I, discuss how the witches tempt Macbeth, referring especially to Scene 3, lines 65–69. Have students restate these lines in their own words.

**AUDITORY** Explain to students that when reading a play, reading aloud or acting out the scenes is a useful technique, as it will often help them hear the **tone** of the **dialogue.** Read some scenes aloud; then, have students take turns reading selected scenes aloud. Assign reading parts ahead of time so students may practice before reading to the class.

**LESS PROFICIENT READERS** Preview each scene or act with a brief summary of the action, or let students' first encounter with each act be through an audio- or videotape. Covering an act in two days may be too quick a pace, so consider dividing the play into smaller portions for study.

## Integrating the Language Arts

**STRATEGIC READING** Before students begin reading, review the organization of a play (stage directions, list of **characters, dialogue**) and the format for recording a reference to a particular line, so that they will be able to refer properly to lines and scenes in their discussion and writing. Famil-

*Drama Study Guide: The Tragedy of Macbeth*

iarity with this technique will also allow students to take notes more quickly and easily.

To review how lines are counted, point out that in split lines the number appears only once, even though the line includes the speech of two characters. Note that acts are represented by capital Roman numerals, and line numbers are generally written in Arabic numerals. The scene number may be written in either Arabic or lowercase Roman numerals, but the type of numeral should remain consistent. The act number always appears first, the scene number second, and the line number(s) third.

To practice as a class, read aloud the following list of references. Ask students to write down and locate the reference and to copy the appropriate line.

I.i.10 or I.1.10 ["Fair is foul, and foul is fair."]
I.ii.67 or I.2.67 ["What he hath lost, noble Macbeth hath won."]
I.iii.38 or I.3.38 ["So foul and fair a day I have not seen."]
I.vi.20 or I.6.20 ["We rest your hermits." "Where's the Thane of Cawdor?"]

USAGE   In Act I, Scene 5, line 29, the noun *tidings* is used with a singular verb (*is*). Explain that some nouns that are plural in form are sometimes understood as singular in meaning. Some other examples are *checkers, news,* and *whereabouts.* Ask students to look up all four words in the dictionary and determine the verb form(s) required. [*Tidings*—generally plural; *news*—singular; *checkers*—singular, although plural for individual pieces; *whereabouts*—singular or plural.]

SPEAKING AND LISTENING   Discuss with students the differences between reading a story aloud and reading a play aloud, focusing on characterization through speech. Review elements of speech such as pitch, tone, articulation, accent, and pace. Assign specific passages to students, and have them practice on their own before reading their passages aloud in class. Remind them that you expect them to use the elements of speech mentioned above to dramatize their prepared readings.

## Cooperative Learning

THEMATIC AWARENESS   Divide the class into four groups, letting each group choose one of the following **themes: (1)** what it means to be a man; **(2)** the relationship between humans and nature; **(3)** blood; **(4)** opposites.

Have each group follow its theme through the play, identifying pertinent lines and making notes of the developing patterns. Periodically each group should report its findings to the class.

## Classroom Management

READING ALOUD   To involve all students in the process of reading the text aloud, use groups for in-class readings, assigning parts to each student to make sure that everybody gets several chances to read. Each group can simultaneously read aloud the assigned section of text. On the chalkboard, list stopping points at which the group should pause to summarize what has occurred in the passage.

RE-READING   Because much of the thematic content of this play is understood through echoes of previously stated material, re-reading is essential for comprehension. Encourage students to be alert for connections, to take the time to search for lines that are echoed, and to use note cards or self-sticking notes to keep track of themes and connections. Encourage them to re-read the whole play at least once after they have studied it piecemeal and to record a journal entry on how this final reading differs from earlier readings.

## Crossing the Curriculum

SOCIAL SCIENCES   Have students locate Holinshed's work, or use *The Arden Shakespeare,* which contains a large portion of Holinshed's version as an appendix. After reading, they can compare Holinshed's account with the play. They may wish to use a Venn diagram or a different graphic organizer to represent the similarities and differences they find.

ART   Have students make a mask of one of the character's faces to show what feelings that **character** might convey. Students can use construction paper, plaster of Paris, or other materials. Have them wear their masks to act out scenes appropriate to the characters they have represented.

ARCHITECTURE   Encourage students to research Scottish castles and their locales. Students might be particularly interested to find out whether there is a castle at Inverness and, if so, what it is like. After they do their research, suggest that they re-read Act I, Scenes 6 and 7, and draw a blueprint of the rooms involved in the scenes.

## Problem Solving/Critical Thinking

ANALYZING REACTIONS   In Act I, both Macbeth and Banquo encounter the witches. To Macbeth this experience is a temptation to evil, but Banquo does not seem to experience it in the same way. Ask students to use a Venn diagram and brainstorm to find reasons why the two characters might react differently to the same situation. After stu-

*Drama Study Guide: The Tragedy of Macbeth*

HRW MATERIAL COPYRIGHTED UNDER NOTICE APPEARING EARLIER IN THIS WORK.

25

dents complete the diagram, ask them whether any general conclusions about these two characters can be drawn.

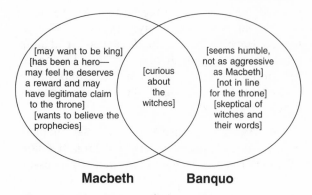

**Macbeth**   **Banquo**

## Professional Notes

**CULTURAL DIVERSITY**   Point out that Shakespeare was writing about witches for an audience that may have believed in them. Allow students an opportunity to discuss how other writers and film directors have portrayed witches, such as those in fairy tales or in movies like *The Wizard of Oz.*

**CRITICAL COMMENT: DRAMA**   Allow students to consider the following comments quoted in J. L. Styan's *The Elements of Drama:*

> [The critic] Granville-Barker asks us to envisage the task before the reader: "He must, so to speak, perform the whole play in his imagination; as he reads, each effect must come home to him; the succession and contrast of scenes, the harmony and clash of the music of the dialogue, the action implied, the mere physical opposition of characters, or the silent figure standing aloof—for that also can be eloquent."

. . . Leave your armchair throne of judgment, says Granville-Barker, submit for the while to be tossed to and fro in the action of the play: Drama's first aim is to subdue us.

From *The Elements of Drama* by J. L. Styan. Copyright © 1960 by **Cambridge University Press.** Reprinted by permission of the publisher.

## Assessment Tools

### CHECK TEST: QUESTIONS AND ANSWERS

1. In Act I, Scene 2, why does King Duncan give Macbeth a new title? [To reward him for bravery.]
2. What do the witches predict for Macbeth and Banquo? [Macbeth will become Thane of Cawdor and king; Banquo will father kings.]
3. When the audience first meets Lady Macbeth, what is she doing? [Reading a letter from Macbeth.]
4. Whom does Duncan name as Prince of Cumberland? [His son Malcolm.]
5. In the final scene of this act, what is the **conflict** between Lady Macbeth and Macbeth? [Whether or not to kill Duncan.]

**INFORMAL ASSESSMENT**   To check that students are using the language of the play to respond to questions and to participate in class discussion, rate them on a scale of one to five (five points being the best), using the following three criteria:

1   Uses important words from the play (for example, theme words).
2   Quotes lines from the play when appropriate.
3   Uses citations correctly.

# Act II

## Strategies for Inclusion

**ENGLISH LANGUAGE DEVELOPMENT**   Discuss the meaning of *motive,* and help students determine which characters might have a motive to kill Duncan. Lead students to understand, for example, that Malcolm and Donalbain, as Duncan's heirs, may have a motive. Have students re-read, in pairs, the **dialogue** in Scene 3 between Malcolm and Donalbain (starting with line 135) and answer these questions: What do these characters think about what has happened? What do they think about their own safety? What is said in Scene 4, lines 24–29, that confirms their fears?

**INTRAPERSONAL**   Remind students that although the play glosses over the murder by placing it off-stage, Macbeth is about to take a human life. Ask them to think about Duncan, who is about to be murdered in his sleep, and to jot down a few notes about the feelings they have about him as a king and as a human being. Ask them to work their ideas into epitaphs and to share them with the class.

**KINESTHETIC**   Assign particular scenes to groups of two to four students, and ask the groups to perform their scenes as either skits or puppet shows. Puppets can be made by backing pictures from magazines with poster board and gluing the cutout figures to wooden sticks.

*Drama Study Guide: The Tragedy of Macbeth*

# Cooperative Learning

**RESEARCH**   Divide the class into groups of three to five students to look up and share information about the specific historical references in *Macbeth*. Possible topics are the family trees of Macbeth and Lady Macbeth, showing their relationship to royalty; maps or specific information on the locations mentioned in the text; or the actual chronology of historical events as compared with the events in *Macbeth*. Invite groups to create a presentation to share their information with the rest of the class.

# Integrating the Language Arts

**STRATEGIC READING**   To help students read more carefully and interpret as they read, encourage them to summarize in their Reader's Logs the tone and meaning of each scene. Invite them to discuss their summaries and to select the best wording to post on a bulletin board as a review of the action, scene by scene.

**WRITING: ESSAY**   Have students write an in-class paper supporting the following thesis statement: Shakespeare's use of nature imagery reinforces Macbeth's unnatural killing of King Duncan. Students must use at least three quotations from Act I or Act II to develop their arguments.

**MECHANICS**   Have students study the text to find devices that Shakespeare uses to add syllables to, or subtract them from, words to make a ten-syllable line. Invite students to rewrite a fairy tale in lines of ten syllables, using some of the devices Shakespeare uses to make the language fit the format. [Devices include contractions, grave accents, and changes in word form.]

**LANGUAGE AND VOCABULARY**   As a class, analyze a short passage, identifying individual words that are not in use today or whose meanings are different now. List each word on the chalkboard, and beside each, have students suggest a more modern word. Re-read the passage, substituting the modern words, and ask for students' responses to the changed sound of the language.

# Classroom Management

**USING FILMS**   If you use videos to augment your teaching of *Macbeth*, decide what role you want the films to have. Will you use them to introduce material? to reinforce material? as a culminating experience? Be aware that some students' own images will be overwhelmed by those of a film. Also, it is often worthwhile to present at least portions from more than one film, because one film alone can seem authoritative to students, leading them to believe that it embodies the "correct" interpretation of the play.

**QUESTION SLIPS**   Give students an opportunity to write down anonymously any questions concerning things they do not understand about the play. This can help you clear up misconceptions that do not surface in class discussion.

# Crossing the Curriculum

**SOCIAL SCIENCES**   Have students research the rules for succession to the thrones in Scotland and England. Encourage them to create a chart to show comparisons between these rules (and the reasons behind them).

**SCIENCE**   Have students brainstorm in groups to provide natural explanations for the occurrences mentioned in Act II, Scene 3, lines 52–59, and Scene 4, lines 1–18. Ask each group to write a brief report detailing its explanations. [For example, for the first reference, an earthquake could cause chimneys to crumble, cries of fear, and shaking of the earth—perhaps just coincident with Duncan's murder.]

# Problem Solving/Critical Thinking

**LOOKING FOR CLUES**   Explain that just as police investigators or psychologists may analyze a person, so literary scholars analyze a **character's** thought process and actions by looking critically for clues. Have students review passages of the text related to Duncan's murder. Based on the evidence so far, have them determine who is responsible for Duncan's murder: Is it the result of Macbeth's choice, the witches' curse, or manipulation by other characters? In a class discussion, students should defend their answers with references from the text.

# Professional Notes

**THEMATIC CONNECTIONS: "UNDER A HAND ACCURSED"**   Ask students why this might be an appropriate title for a discussion of this play. [Possible responses: It is a line spoken by Lennox (Act III, Scene 6, line 49) and refers to Scotland suffering under a ruler who has committed murder. Perhaps the phrase refers to the curses of the witches, suggesting that Macbeth's actions were fated. It might be purposefully ambiguous, so that readers will stop to consider whether events are influenced by choice or fate.]

*Drama Study Guide: **The Tragedy of Macbeth***

HRW MATERIAL COPYRIGHTED UNDER NOTICE APPEARING EARLIER IN THIS WORK.

27

# Assessment Tools

## CHECK TEST: QUESTIONS AND ANSWERS

1. How does Duncan die? [Macbeth stabs him.]

2. Why doesn't Lady Macbeth do it? [The sleeping Duncan reminds her of her father.]

3. What does Lady Macbeth do to make others seem guilty? [She smears blood on the sleeping grooms.]

4. Immediately after Duncan dies, Macbeth hears a voice cry out. What does it say Macbeth has murdered? [Sleep.]

5. Who flees the castle in fear? [Duncan's sons, Malcolm and Donalbain.]

## OBSERVATION ASSESSMENT: READING

As students discuss **themes** revealed in Acts I and II, note whether they are making specific references to echoes and repetitions in the text. The following scale may help you evaluate students.

1 Discusses text generally or inaccurately.

2 Speaks generally with some mention of lines or scenes.

3 Refers to lines or scenes without citing specific references.

4 Occasionally cites specific references to support discussion.

5 Frequently cites specific references to support discussion.

## Connecting with *Macbeth*

Explain that De Quincey presents an argument with proposed solutions, some of which are dismissed based on further evidence. After students read "Macbeth's Porter" and De Quincey's essay in the HRW Classics edition of *Macbeth* (pages 123–124 and 132–134), have them use the following chart to summarize and evaluate various theories about the inclusion of the knocking, based on the ideas presented by the critics and the students' own thoughts about the scene.

| Purpose of the Knocking at the Gate | | |
|---|---|---|
| Possible Cause for Including the Porter [to create a disturbance] | Reason for Dismissal of Cause [play loses intensity] | Reason for Acceptance of Cause [brings Macbeth back to reality] |

# Act III

## Strategies for Inclusion

**ENGLISH LANGUAGE DEVELOPMENT** To help students keep focused on the **plot,** have them keep a time line of the actions that take place. Pause periodically to review what has happened in the play.

**MUSICAL** Ask students to rewrite Hecate's speech (Act III, Scene 5, lines 2–35) as a rap song. Have them pay particular attention to their word choice and rhythm. After they have had a chance to share their songs with the class, ask them to return to the original speech and analyze its word choices and rhythm, noting the downbeats that give it a singsong feel.

## Integrating the Language Arts

**STRATEGIC READING** Assign pairs of students to use reciprocal teaching to aid text comprehension. As the students read a passage aloud, one student asks questions that arise during the reading, and the second student answers as many questions as possible. Then, after an assigned number of lines, they reverse roles. At the end of each scene, in a short paragraph in their Reader's Logs, both students should summarize what they understand. Briefly model the process before students begin.

**WRITING: PSYCHOLOGIST'S REPORT ON MACBETH** Brainstorm with students about Macbeth's thoughts and motivations in Act III, noting all ideas on the chalkboard. Then, have students write a psychologist's report on Macbeth, answering the following questions: Is he completely in control of his mind? Is he hallucinating from the guilt he feels, or does he really see things that others do not see? Why does he continue to plot additional murders? In their report, students should cite specific references to support their diagnoses.

**SPEAKING AND LISTENING** Have a student read his or her favorite lines from the play. A second student should then volunteer favorite lines and relate them to the lines read by the first student. A third student should read and relate to the second student, and so on. Students may identify similarities, differences, changes over time, echoes, and repetitions.

*Drama Study Guide: **The Tragedy of Macbeth***

# Cooperative Learning

**CHARACTER SOCIOGRAMS** Have students work in groups of three or four to create character sociograms—graphics with symbols and words that show the relationships among characters. Challenge students to include all the characters they have read about in the play so far and to be creative in the kind of symbols they produce to show how each character relates to the others.

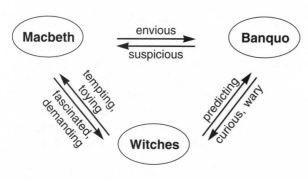

# Classroom Management

**FIELDING QUESTIONS** Put up a large sheet of kraft paper on which students can write questions as they read, leaving room between questions for other students to answer. Periodically check to make sure that misconceptions are cleared up. Leave a few minutes at the beginning or the end of class to discuss the posted questions and answers or to allow students to add or answer questions. Once questions are written and answered on the kraft paper, keep notes on interpretations that may change as students encounter additional information in the text. Remind them that as new clues to the material surface, readers must rethink or expand their interpretations. (For example, speculation about Lady Macbeth's children must also take into account Act IV, Scene 3, line 216, which students have not yet read.)

# Crossing the Curriculum

**SOCIAL SCIENCES** Students may note with uneasiness that as of Act III, Scene 1, line 10, Banquo has not yet acted on his suspicions. Ask students to research this question: What support should Banquo have for his suspicions before he brings an accusation? Encourage them to consider laws about bringing charges for murder and also the standards of proof required to convict a person of murder. Ask them whether, given these laws, Banquo should act now or wait. Have them present an oral investigative report such as they might hear on a news broadcast, including the pertinent information they find and applying it to the text.

**PERFORMING ARTS** Banquo's ghost presents some interesting staging challenges. Assign stu-

dents to groups of four or five, and have them stage the scene in which Banquo's ghost appears to Macbeth. Students may find it helpful to learn about the treatment of other famous ghosts in the performing arts, such as the one in *Hamlet*. Remind them that techniques used in film often will not work in live performance; however, the Globe Theater, where Shakespeare's work was often performed, had a trapdoor.

# Professional Notes

**CRITICAL COMMENT: PUBLIC AND PRIVATE** According to the critic J. L. Styan, "Shakespeare's *Macbeth* is another play, touching the opposition of the public and the private world and the consequent horrors of a divided mind." Ask students to interpret the play in terms of Macbeth's separation of the public and the private. [Possible response: In his mind, Macbeth knows the evil he has done, but publicly he tries to hide his deeds and feelings in order to maintain his position. This internal struggle causes him even more anguish than he already feels for murdering Duncan.]

From *The Elements of Drama* by J. L. Styan. Copyright © 1960 by *Cambridge University Press*. Reprinted by permission of the publisher.

**CULTURAL DIVERSITY** At Macbeth's banquet the guests would sit in order of rank. Have students brainstorm to come up with modern settings in which sitting by rank is still important. [Sample responses: The U.S. Senate, courtrooms, weddings, funerals, and some formal business meetings.]

# Assessment Tools

**CHECK TEST: QUESTIONS AND ANSWERS**
1. Why is Macbeth determined to have Fleance killed? [So Banquo's sons will never rule.]
2. Whom do the murderers kill? [Banquo.]
3. Who escapes? [Fleance.]
4. What does Macbeth see at the banquet? [The ghost of Banquo.]
5. What are Macduff and Malcolm doing in England? [Securing an army to overthrow Macbeth.]

**SELF-REFLECTION** Ask students to review and summarize briefly their use of each of the following strategies, using a scale of one through five (five being the best) to indicate their level of competence in each task: (**1**) visualizing the scenes; (**2**) re-reading for specific references to support their points; (**3**) using the Reader's Log to get questions answered. Hold short conferences with students to discuss their self-assessments.

*Drama Study Guide: **The Tragedy of Macbeth***

HRW MATERIAL COPYRIGHTED UNDER NOTICE APPEARING EARLIER IN THIS WORK.

29

# Act IV

## Strategies for Inclusion

**ENGLISH LANGUAGE DEVELOPMENT**   Help students define the word *traitor* by asking the following questions: How might someone be a traitor to his or her country? [Sample response: By sharing information that would hurt the country.] to one's family? [Sample response: By refusing to help the family.] Before students read Scene 2, ask them how they think Lady Macduff will feel about her husband's leaving Scotland. After they have read the scene, discuss whether Macduff is a traitor or whether there are other explanations for his behavior.

**BODILY-KINESTHETIC**   Divide the class into two teams. Each team should prepare and then pose in five "frozen scenes." If the other team guesses the scene being represented on the first try, the presenting team gets five points. If the other team guesses it on the second try, the presenting team gets two; on the third try, one point. The team with the most points wins. Remind students to present material the audience sees. They cannot, for example, show Duncan being murdered.

**VISUAL/AUDITORY**   If possible, have students work in small groups to create a computer-animated scene with sound. Each group should choose a short portion of a scene from the play. One student might be in charge of getting information on how the technology works; another might do the artwork; another might plan the animation; another might create the sound.

## Integrating the Language Arts

**WRITING: NOVEL EXCERPT**   Have students work in small groups or singly to translate a portion of *Macbeth* into an excerpt from a novel. Ask them to read their excerpts aloud, and discuss as a class how reading a novel is different from reading a play.

**LANGUAGE AND VOCABULARY**   After students finish reading Act IV, ask them to return to earlier acts to identify lines that they understand differently now that they are used to Shakespeare's language and have new information that requires revision in their thinking. Ask them to list words that they find have layers of meaning. Then, have them develop some of these key words into collages that show possible interpretations.

**SPEAKING AND LISTENING**   Ask each student to choose a **character** from *Macbeth* and write an introduction as if he or she were introducing that character as the guest speaker for a banquet. Remind students that introductions can be serious or humorous. Have them deliver their introductions in a formal manner. Encourage them to dramatize their brief speeches with appropriate pauses, inflection, and enunciation.

## Cooperative Learning

**CREATING A DANCE**   Have students work in groups of three or four to create a dance for the song mentioned in the stage directions of Act IV, Scene 1, after line 43. They should consider mood and atmosphere as they choreograph steps and select accompanying music. Provide an opportunity for the dances to be performed for an audience.

**PUZZLERS**   Divide the class into groups of three students, and have the groups analyze the prophecies of the apparitions. Ask them to make notes on what they think each apparition means and why the apparitions take the forms that they take. Have them return to these notes after the final act to compare their thoughts at this point with their thoughts then.

## Classroom Management

**FINDING PRACTICE SPACE**   When planning dramatic readings or dances, arrange for rehearsal space that will allow students to practice without interference from others. Investigate the possibility of using a large room, such as the school cafeteria or the auditorium, where groups can move about easily.

**MANAGING THE READER'S RESPONSE CLASSROOM**   When posing questions for discussion, allow plenty of time for students to consider a question and formulate a response. Allowing all students time to think promotes their comfort in speaking to large groups and gives everyone a chance to formulate an answer.

## Crossing the Curriculum

**ART**   Have students work in groups of four to create a piece of scenery for the play. Its design should reflect a thoughtful interpretation of its role in the play. Assign each student a leadership role: an artist (to direct the painting or drawing), a production manager (to oversee the collection of necessary building materials), a director (to compare the details noted in the play with the group's rendering of the scenery), and a stage manager (to consider placement and use of the scenery).

*Drama Study Guide: **The Tragedy of Macbeth***

**SOCIAL SCIENCES** Have interested students prepare a debate on whether Macbeth actually sees the apparitions in Act IV. Assign students to two teams to research the subject of parapsychology (a branch of psychology that investigates psychic phenomena) and plan their strategy in refuting or supporting Macbeth's sightings. At debate time, flip a coin to see which team begins and alternate between the teams at one-minute intervals until each team member has made a point. Let the class discuss who they believe won the debate and why.

**HEALTH** Students may be interested in finding out more about the king's "touch" and the disease that it was supposed to cure (scrofula). Encourage them to research both contemporary and current understandings of this phenomenon. Have them present a short oral report to the class on their findings.

## Problem Solving/Critical Thinking

**EASING THE BLOW** Being the bearer of bad news can be a difficult and uncomfortable job. Have students list actions, approaches, or strategies that the speaker can use to lessen the discomfort of the situation. Ask them to consider the following questions: Is a leading statement—such as "I'm really sorry, but I have bad news for you"—helpful? Should you ever just blurt out the news? Should you use euphemisms? What can or should you do after the message is delivered? Ask students to share ideas and determine whether some of their strategies might have helped Ross convey the bad news to Macduff.

## Professional Notes

**CULTURAL DIVERSITY** People suffer from guilt for things they purposely did and knew were wrong, as well as for mistakes and accidents; and they handle guilt in different ways. Some religions account for the need to deal with guilt through penance, confessions, and prayer. Some people relieve guilt by discussing their feelings with friends or health professionals.

**THEMATIC CONNECTIONS: "UNDER A HAND ACCURSED"** Now that students have learned more about how Macbeth acted after the witches' first predictions, they may feel themselves equipped to discuss the question, What is a curse? in conjunction with the notion that Scotland was "under a hand accursed." They might discuss the topics of free will (the belief that actions are the choice of individuals), predestination (fate), and determinism (the concept that everything, even individual choices, results from a series of causes) as shown in this play.

## Assessment Tools

### CHECK TEST: FILL-IN-THE-BLANK

1. When the second witch says "Something wicked this way comes," she is referring to _____. [Macbeth]

2. The second apparition says that Macbeth cannot be harmed by _____. [anyone born of a woman]

3. The third apparition says that Macbeth will not be vanquished until Birnam Wood _____. [comes to Dunsinane]

4. Lady Macduff and all her children are murdered by_____. [killers hired by Macbeth]

5. Malcolm tests Macduff's loyalty to Scotland by pretending to _____. [Sample responses: be evil; be lustful, greedy, and bent on destruction; be worse than Macbeth]

**ONGOING ASSESSMENT** To see whether students are following the **themes** that run through the acts, ask them to write a one-page paper identifying and explaining one of the themes of the play. Students should discuss any **symbols** associated with the theme and refer to dialogue or scenes that reflect the theme. The following scale may help you score these assignments:

1 Theme is not well defined or supported.

2 Theme is stated; needs clearer support.

3 Theme is defined; support is adequate.

4 Theme is precisely defined; support is thorough.

# Act V

## Strategies for Inclusion

**ADVANCED** Have interested students compare the historical Macbeth with the Shakespearean character. From their research, have them compose a letter from Shakespeare to his audience, defending the changes he made when writing the play.

**INTRAPERSONAL** As students consider the decision-making process that leads Macbeth to his

*Drama Study Guide: The Tragedy of Macbeth*

death, have them complete an Options Tree. They should start with Macbeth's decision about whether to believe the witches' initial predictions and trace the path he follows through each decision he faces. Ask students to speculate in their Reader's Logs about how different things might have been if, for example, Macbeth had decided not to murder Duncan.

Hide in the castle     Fight Macduff

Murder Macduff's family     Avoid urge to retaliate

Believe apparitions     Be cautious

Have Banquo murdered     Let Banquo's sons be king

Kill Duncan     Wait to see

Believe predictions/Disregard

**LESS PROFICIENT READERS** As the class works through this final act, pause periodically to help students make the connections between the **resolutions** found in Act V and earlier **foreshadowing.** For example, point out the way the prophecies come true, and ask students whether they have guessed these riddles. Ask whether, in hindsight, there are any clues in previous acts that Lady Macbeth is disturbed enough to end her life or whether Lennox's earlier lines hint that he might turn against Macbeth.

**SPECIAL NEEDS** Ask students to consider why people still study *Macbeth* today. Guide them with the following questions: Did you learn anything from the downfall of Macbeth? Were there any **characters** you strongly liked or disliked, and why? What was Macbeth's flaw? Can you think of any modern political situations that are similar to this one?

## Integrating the Language Arts

**STRATEGIC READING** To review and reinforce the chronology of the story, divide the class into three or four groups of students after everyone has finished reading the play. Have one student in each group read or recite a memorable or important line or sentence from the play. Other students in the group should try to identify the speaker and circumstances. Let students take turns reading lines to the group and guessing.

**WRITING: NEWSPAPERS** Have students work in groups of four or five to create a newspaper based on the incident in *Macbeth*. Each student should contribute at least one article, and each should perform the additional task of editor, typist, artist, or layout designer. Remind students to use quotations from the play in their writing. Besides articles that cover the major events in the play, students may want to contribute extra features, such as sidebars, captioned pictures, opinion features or letters to the editor, classified ads, an astrological forecast, a weather report, or a travel guide.

**LANGUAGE AND VOCABULARY** Have students work in pairs to characterize Lady Macbeth's language in the sleepwalking scene, prompted by the following questions: **(1)** How is her language here different from her language elsewhere? **(2)** How would you describe the sentence length and construction? **(3)** Where in time and space does she think she is?

**SPEAKING AND LISTENING** To help students hear the **meter,** have them try the following approach: **(1)** Figure out whether a line is iambic pentameter or tetrameter; **(2)** read the line as if it were absolutely true to the meter, noting where the regular accents on the words come out wrong; **(3)** correct the reading for accents. Students should keep in mind that actors deliver lines differently, varying the tempo, pitch, and pauses. Once they have practiced, let students read their favorite speeches to the class.

## Cooperative Learning

**DIRECTORS FOR A DAY** Divide the class into small groups, and have students imagine they are directing a production of *Macbeth*. Ask them to choose one scene and write directions for characterization, timing, blocking, costuming, and sound effects.

**BLOCK SCHEDULING** The longer class period provides an opportunity for students to engage in various elements of drama. Read a scene aloud in class (twenty to thirty minutes). After discussion, reinforce the elements of drama by allowing students to work in groups to perform the scene (forty-five to sixty minutes). Allow time for prop gathering, set placement, room rearrangement, and so on. If possible, take the class to the auditorium to provide a feel for performing on a stage.

**ON-LINE GROUP PROJECTS** Exchange ideas with others teaching *Macbeth* by posting a request on an English-teaching listserv for collaborative projects.

## Crossing the Curriculum

**HEALTH** Students may be interested in studying sleepwalking. Have them research the main causes of sleepwalking and current approaches to curing the problem. Ask them to design a poster to share their findings.

*Drama Study Guide: **The Tragedy of Macbeth***

**PSYCHOLOGY** This play is also about a marriage that is tested and found wanting. After students have read the play, let them act as marriage counselors. Ask them to make references to the miscommunication they see between the Macbeths or to stage directions that describe the Macbeths' relationship. Then, have students work in groups of three, assuming the roles of counselor, Lady Macbeth, and Macbeth, and let them role-play the counseling session. Ask the students in each group to determine whether this marriage can be saved and to defend their answers in a class discussion with references from the text.

**SOCIAL SCIENCES** Some students may wish to focus on the battle strategies in the text and in Holinshed's history. Ask students to write a series of diary entries from a soldier's point of view or to create a diorama showing the battle plans.

# Professional Notes

**CULTURAL DIVERSITY** Have students work in pairs to learn how various countries celebrate a government leader's taking office. Assign one country to each pair, and have them find answers to the following questions: What title does the head of state use? Where is the ceremony held? Who attends? Who presides? What promises, if any, does the new officeholder make? Is there a religious element to the ceremony? Students should research the symbolism, costumes, and wording used in the ceremonies and report their findings to the class.

**CRITICAL COMMENT: THE WITCHES** The critic Willard Farnham discusses the role of the witches:

> Before we make up our minds about the guilt of the hero and, finally, the meaning of the tragedy, we must first decide what power these beings wield over the actions and fortunes of the hero. They are witches having the forms of repulsive old women, but they are not mortal witches such as the law might get its hands upon and put to death in the England or Scotland of Shakespeare's day. They are "weird sisters," but the word *weird* as applied to them cannot mean that they have control of Macbeth's destiny and compel him to do all that he does. Macbeth is certainly no mere puppet moving under their manipulation. Nothing is clearer than that Shakespeare writes of Macbeth as of a man who has free will so far, at least, as the choice of good or evil is concerned and who in choosing evil creates for himself physical misfortune and a spiritual hell on earth. In what they do, the witches show themselves to have a power over Macbeth that is

limited, however strong it may be. They are supernatural agents of evil, and in working to make fair into foul, they reveal both the capacities and the incapacities that the Christian tradition has attributed to devils. They tempt Macbeth to do evil and tempt him with great subtlety. They cannot force him to do it.

From "The Witches" from *Shakespeare's Tragic Frontier* by Willard Farnham. Copyright © 1950 by **Blackwell Publishers.** Reprinted by permission of the publisher.

**CRITICAL COMMENT: PLOT** Ask students to discuss this analysis by Terence Eagleton:

> *Macbeth* centers around a single action—the murder of Duncan—which . . . is seen as self-defeating. The whole structure of the play makes this clear: Scotland moves from health to sickness and back into health, Malcolm replaces Duncan, and the wheel comes full circle without Macbeth having made any permanent achievement. The energy he expends in trying to secure his position contrasts ironically with this lack of attainment: His actions are canceled out by the circular movement of the play, and he becomes a momentary aberration in Scotland's history, an aberration without lasting consequence: The history rights itself and continues.

From *Shakespeare and Society* by Terence Eagleton. Copyright © 1967 by Terence Eagleton. Reprinted by permission of **Chatto and Windus, an imprint of Random House UK Ltd.**

[Students may agree that Macbeth himself recognized this when he spoke of "a tale told by an idiot, signifying nothing." Or they may say that whatever Malcolm achieves will be partly due to this "aberration"—perhaps Malcolm will be a better king than he might have been had he inherited the throne earlier, without the experiences that made him learn to be wary, unlike his trusting father.]

# Assessment Tools

## CHECK TEST: QUESTIONS AND ANSWERS

1. Name two important actions that Lady Macbeth performs while sleepwalking. [Sample responses: She rubs her hands as if washing; writes a letter; speaks, implicating herself and Macbeth in the murders of Duncan, Banquo, and Lady Macduff.]

2. Macbeth has been planning to let the English besiege his castle, but after the report that Birnam Wood is moving, how do his plans change? [He decides to go out and fight.]

3. What choice does Macduff give Macbeth? [Fight or yield and be imprisoned and put on display so the public can mock him.]

*Drama Study Guide: **The Tragedy of Macbeth***

HRW MATERIAL COPYRIGHTED UNDER NOTICE APPEARING EARLIER IN THIS WORK.

33

**4.** Who becomes the new king of Scotland? [Malcolm.]

**PEER EVALUATION**  As students complete group activities, ask them to rate their group's performance on a scale of one to five (five being the best rating) on each of the following criteria:

**1**  Reads with expression and characterization when quoting the text.

**2**  Supports ideas with quotations from the text.

**3**  Makes connections between different parts of the text.

*Drama Study Guide: **The Tragedy of Macbeth***

# Plot Synopsis

## Act I

### Scene 1

Three witches, the weird sisters, plan to meet Macbeth later the same day.

### Scene 2

At an army camp, a captain reports to the Scottish king, Duncan, that Macbeth has killed the traitor Macdonwald in a battle with the Norwegians. The Norwegians, faced with the fury of the Scottish captains Banquo and Macbeth, ask for peace. Duncan decides, unknown to Macbeth, to give Macbeth the title Thane of Cawdor. The king then condemns to death the present Thane of Cawdor.

### Scene 3

On a heath, Macbeth and Banquo meet the three witches, who make three predictions: One witch calls Macbeth Thane of Cawdor; another says that Macbeth will be king; and the third says that Banquo will beget kings but will not be one himself. Two Scottish noblemen, Ross and Angus, tell Macbeth that he has been made Thane of Cawdor. Macbeth takes the witches' prophecies seriously and begins to have disturbing thoughts.

### Scene 4

At his palace at Forres, King Duncan proclaims his son Malcolm heir to the throne. Macbeth broods on his black desires.

### Scene 5

At the Macbeths' castle at Inverness, Lady Macbeth learns of the witches' prophecies through a letter from her husband and, fearing that he is too weak to seize the throne himself, begins to plot Macbeth's reign as king. A messenger tells her that King Duncan will visit their castle that night. She tells Macbeth that they should take the opportunity to kill the king.

### Scene 6

Duncan arrives at Macbeth's castle, along with his sons Malcolm and Donalbain and the noblemen Banquo, Ross, Angus, Lennox, and Macduff. The king comments with dramatic irony on the pleasant air in Macbeth's home. Lady Macbeth graciously welcomes the king while plotting his murder.

### Scene 7

Macbeth speaks his first important soliloquy, explaining how his ambition has led him to thoughts of murder. Lady Macbeth encourages her husband to commit the murder.

## Act II

### Scene 1

In his castle, Macbeth comes upon Banquo and Banquo's son Fleance after midnight as they make their way to bed. Macbeth and Banquo talk of the witches' predictions, and Macbeth suggests that he and Banquo meet to talk privately. After Banquo and Fleance leave, Macbeth imagines that he sees a blood-covered dagger. He then leaves to commit the murder.

### Scene 2

Macbeth murders Duncan offstage. Although unable to commit the murder herself because the sleeping Duncan reminds her of her father, Lady Macbeth seems calm yet thrilled by the murder. Macbeth seems deeply troubled and dazed. He hears a voice say that Macbeth has killed sleep. He mistakenly takes the grooms' (the guards') daggers from the room; Lady Macbeth places them beside the sleeping grooms, whom she smears with the king's blood.

### Scene 3

The next morning a drunken porter responds to Macduff's and Lennox's knocking at the gate. Macbeth now appears calm. Macduff discovers Duncan's body while Lennox describes the unnatural occurrences of the night before. The king's sons, Malcolm and Donalbain, flee the country.

Macbeth announces that he killed Duncan's grooms because they murdered the king. Lady Macbeth faints.

## Scene 4

Outside Macbeth's castle, Ross and an Old Man speak of the wild and unnatural events of the night before. Macduff reveals that Macbeth has gone to Scone to be installed as king and that Duncan's sons are suspected of murdering their father. Macduff says that he will not attend Macbeth's coronation, and he dreads the conditions under the new king.

---

# Act III

## Scene 1

At the king's palace at Forres, Banquo reveals that he suspects Macbeth of having murdered Duncan. Macbeth invites Banquo to a banquet that night and learns that Banquo and his son Fleance will come. Macbeth hires three murderers to kill Banquo and Fleance.

## Scene 2

Lady Macbeth expresses her discontent in a brief soliloquy. She urges Macbeth to be fearless and more cheerful. Macbeth says that he envies Duncan, who is at peace, and says that he fears Banquo and his children. He also says that a dreadful deed will soon be accomplished. He tells Lady Macbeth nothing of his plans to have Banquo and Fleance murdered.

## Scene 3

Near the palace the murderers kill Banquo. Fleance escapes.

## Scene 4

The banquet at Forres is under way when one of the murderers calls Macbeth aside to tell him that Banquo is dead but Fleance is not. Macbeth alone among the guests sees Banquo's ghost. He speaks to it, causing the other guests to think he is mad. He and Lady Macbeth say that he is ill, and Lady Macbeth dismisses the guests. Macbeth says that he will send for Macduff and visit the witches.

## Scene 5

At a witches' haunt, Hecate, the queen of the witches, meets the weird sisters and berates them for leaving her out of their dealings with Macbeth.

## Scene 6

A conversation in the palace brings developments up-to-date. Lennox explains his suspicions of Macbeth and asks a Scottish lord where Macduff is now. The lord answers that Macduff is in England, raising an army against Macbeth. Macbeth, he reports, summoned Macduff but Macduff refused to come.

---

# Act IV

## Scene 1

The weird sisters chant before a caldron. Macbeth enters demanding to know the future. The witches show him three apparitions (an armed head, a bloody child, and a child wearing a crown), and these visions give him advice and make predictions. The first tells Macbeth to beware of Macduff; the second says that no one born of a woman will hurt Macbeth; and the third tells him that he will not be conquered until Birnam Wood comes to Dunsinane. When Macbeth demands to learn more, the witches show him another apparition: eight kings, including Banquo, who points to these kings as his descendants and holds up a mirror to indicate the continuation of his line. The witches vanish, and Lennox appears and tells Macbeth that Macduff has fled to England. As the scene ends, Macbeth is planning to murder Lady Macduff, her children, and anyone else of Macduff's lineage.

## Scene 2

At Macduff's castle, Ross tells Lady Macduff that Macduff has gone to England. Ross leaves, and as Lady Macduff and her young son talk, a messenger arrives and warns them to flee. The murderers arrive immediately and kill first her son and then her.

*Drama Study Guide: The Tragedy of Macbeth*

## Scene 3

In England, Macduff attempts to secure Malcolm's aid in fighting Macbeth. Malcolm first tests Macduff's loyalty to Scotland. After Macduff proves his integrity, Malcolm tells him that an army is ready to attack Macbeth. Ross then tells Macduff that his wife, children, and servants have been murdered. Macduff prays to meet Macbeth in battle.

# Act V

## Scene 1

At the castle at Dunsinane, Lady Macbeth's lady-in-waiting and doctor discuss Lady Macbeth's sleepwalking. As they talk, Lady Macbeth enters, walking in her sleep. She rubs her hands repeatedly as if to rid them of the blood that she imagines stains them. From Lady Macbeth's words the onlookers infer that the Macbeths murdered Duncan. The doctor will not speak of his suspicions.

## Scene 2

In Birnam Wood, near Dunsinane, Malcolm, Macduff, and their forces gather. The Scottish lords discuss their plans and Macbeth's reported state of mind.

## Scene 3

Inside the castle at Dunsinane, Macbeth, because of the witches' prophecies, feels confident that he is invincible. A servant brings news of the approaching army.

## Scene 4

The troops have gathered near Birnam Wood to attack Macbeth. Malcolm orders the soldiers to carry branches from the woods as camouflage.

## Scene 5

In the castle at Dunsinane, as Macbeth awaits the approaching army, an offstage cry is heard. Seyton, Macbeth's attendant, enters with news that Lady Macbeth is dead. Macbeth delivers his famous soliloquy ("Tomorrow, and tomorrow, and tomorrow . . ."). A messenger brings the news that Birnam Wood is approaching the castle.

## Scene 6

On the field near the castle, Malcolm orders his troops to throw down their camouflage and attack.

## Scene 7

Elsewhere on the field, Macbeth kills Young Siward, son of Siward, the earl of Northumberland. Macbeth exits with Macduff in pursuit.

## Scene 8

Elsewhere on the field, Macduff confronts Macbeth, who at first refuses to fight him, warning him that no one born of a woman can harm him. Macduff explains that he was not born of a woman but by Caesarean section. Macbeth still refuses to fight, but Macduff goads him by vowing to place him in a cage and display him as a fallen tyrant. Their fight begins and continues offstage. Ross reports to Siward that Young Siward has died bravely. Macduff returns with the head of Macbeth and acclaims Malcolm king of Scotland. Malcolm promises to restore peace and order to Scotland.

*Drama Study Guide: The Tragedy of Macbeth*

HRW MATERIAL COPYRIGHTED UNDER NOTICE APPEARING EARLIER IN THIS WORK.

37

# Guided Reading

The questions and comments that follow focus on the staging, characterization, and plot development of the play. They ask students for opinions and comments and are designed to help students think about and respond to the play as they read it. They correspond to specific lines in the play and are followed by answers or sample responses. You may want to use these questions and comments to help students who are having difficulty with the play; they provide the reader with an opportunity to stop and catch up on the plot or understand the thinking of a particular character.

## Act I   Scene 1

**LINE 2.** *This scene, played against thunder and lightning, sets the mood of the play. The witches might have made their appearance through the trapdoor on the stage. Thunder would have been produced by rolling cannonballs in the area above the stage. How might these actresses (actors in Shakespeare's day) convey a sense of menace?*

**ANSWER.** They might use movement (awkward or ritualistic), voice (unnatural pitch and cackling laughs), costumes, and makeup.

## Scene 2

**LINE 7.** *The captain is bloody and could be carried in or supported by others. How would he speak his lines?*

**ANSWER.** The captain might gasp from weakness but speak urgently to convey the good news.

**LINE 23.** *Notice that this horrible action is described by a messenger, not shown onstage. What has Macbeth done to the rebellious Macdonwald?*

**ANSWER.** Macbeth has slashed Macdonwald open from navel to jaws, beheaded him, and stuck the head atop the castle wall.

**LINE 35.** *This line can be delivered in several ways. How do you imagine the captain speaks it?*

**ANSWER.** He might speak ironically or admiringly.

**LINE 44.** *Duncan can be played in several ways: as a strong but aging king, as a frail old man, as a foolish old man who doesn't understand what's going on. As the play goes on, decide how you interpret Duncan's character.*

**ANSWER.** Students may come to see Duncan as a man who trusts too easily and is naive about reading character. They may suspect personal weakness as they reflect on his failure to lead his troops.

**LINE 67.** *As you continue to read, notice how events will relate to the king's words here. How would you have him say these lines?*

**ANSWER.** He might speak robustly, as if proud to bestow his praise on Macbeth.

## Scene 3

**LINE 38.** *What words is Macbeth echoing here? Why, given the weather, does Macbeth think the day is "fair"?*

**ANSWER.** Remind students that Macbeth has not heard these lines before but is unwittingly echoing the witches' comment in Act I, Scene 1, line 10. Macbeth may consider the day fair because of the victories he achieved. He may be referring to bad weather and a wonderful victory, or he may mean that the killing of Macdonwald and the defeat of Sweno were foul but having succeeded has made the day fair.

**LINE 39.** *What should Banquo do as he sees the witches? How should his voice change between the words* Forres *and* What?

**ANSWER.** Banquo might step back and reach for his sword or raise his hand to ward the witches off. He might gasp or sound surprised as he completes his casual question only to be confronted by such a strange trio.

**LINE 51.** *Banquo's words give a clue as to how Macbeth reacts to the witches. What is his reaction? When Banquo asks "Are ye fantastical . . . ?" (line 53), whom is he addressing?*

*Drama Study Guide: **The Tragedy of Macbeth***

ANSWER. Macbeth is startled. He might show this by the expression on his face or by a gesture of surprise. Banquo is addressing the witches.

**? LINE 61.** *What does Banquo ask the witches?*

ANSWER. Banquo asks them to foretell his future, too, if they can.

**? LINE 71.** *Sinel is Macbeth's father. What do you think Macbeth's tone is here? Is he overeager or just casually curious?*

ANSWER. Macbeth might be puzzled, intrigued, or entranced.

**? FOLLOWING LINE 78, STAGE DIRECTION.** *The witches on Shakespeare's stage would have vanished through the trapdoor. Is Banquo, in his next speech, intrigued or disturbed? How does Macbeth feel?*

ANSWER. Banquo might be puzzled, disturbed, or intrigued. Macbeth is curious to hear more.

**? LINE 117.** Behind *here means "to follow." How should this important aside be spoken? What is Macbeth's mood?*

ANSWER. He might sound crafty and greedy, hopeful and full of wonder, or just very determined. His mood might be impatience, agitation, or awe.

**? LINE 126.** *How does this speech show Banquo as part of the conscience of the play?*

ANSWER. He advises Macbeth to temper his ambition with caution—appearances may be deceiving, and the witches may mean him harm.

**? FOLLOWING LINE 127, STAGE DIRECTION.** *When a character is delivering an aside, the director or the playwright must arrange for the others onstage to be involved in some way so that it would be natural for them not to notice the character who is speaking. Where onstage should Macbeth go to deliver this important aside? What do you think he means by "swelling act" in line 128? Where are Banquo, Angus, and Ross?*

ANSWER. Macbeth should probably come downstage and face the audience while the other characters—Banquo, Angus, and Ross—remain grouped in conversation upstage. The "swelling act" may suggest the stately music that heralds a king's coming—perhaps Macbeth sees his new title as a sign of his coming kingship.

**? LINE 137.** *What do you suppose Macbeth is thinking of that makes his "seated" (fixed) heart knock at his ribs in an unnatural way?*

ANSWER. Macbeth may be imagining that he will murder Duncan to become king himself.

**? LINE 142.** *How might Macbeth look as Banquo notices him brooding?*

ANSWER. He might look dazed, absorbed, or brooding. (The power of his imagination, as Macbeth himself says, may be rendering him lost to the world.)

**? LINE 145.** *To what does Banquo compare Macbeth and his new honors? Is Banquo's mood different from Macbeth's?*

ANSWER. He compares Macbeth's honors to clothes that are new, not yet broken in. Yes, Banquo seems to have dismissed the witches' comments while Macbeth has taken their words to heart.

## Scene 4

**? LINE 8.** *What does this famous line mean: "nothing in his life / Became him like the leaving it"?*

ANSWER. Sample response: The way he died was the finest, most courageous thing he ever did. This might be taken at face value as showing the courage of his confession and his facing death without fear, or it might be construed as an ironic comment about the quality of his life.

**? LINE 12.** *What does Duncan fail to realize about another face? What irony would you feel here?*

ANSWER. Duncan has revealed his weak spot—he is too trusting and is not a good judge of character. The irony is that even as Duncan is acknowledging his mistake, he is making the same mistake with Macbeth that he made with the previous Thane of Cawdor.

**? LINE 32.** *You know Macbeth's thoughts. How do you feel about him as the king lavishes praise on him? Is the king's reception of Banquo even warmer? How might Macbeth react here?*

ANSWER. Students may hope that seeing the king's trust and acknowledging his praise will cause Macbeth to change, as the other Thane of Cawdor did; or they may think Macbeth is a phony and Duncan's praise is ironic. The king hugs Banquo, but he gives Macbeth the honor of being Thane of Cawdor and speaks of him with greater admiration and respect. Macbeth might be jealous of Banquo, or he might feel that Duncan is treating him as an equal and Banquo as a friend.

*Drama Study Guide: The Tragedy of Macbeth*

HRW MATERIAL COPYRIGHTED UNDER NOTICE APPEARING EARLIER IN THIS WORK.

39

**LINE 35.** *There's a clue in this line that shows how moved the king is. What is the king doing at the words "drops of sorrow"?*

ANSWER. Duncan is wiping away tears of joy.

**LINE 39.** *Who is to inherit Duncan's crown?*

ANSWER. His son Malcolm.

**LINE 53.** *Where in this speech do we begin to hear Macbeth talk in terms of darkness?*

ANSWER. Macbeth speaks of literal darkness by telling the stars to hide their light; he speaks of the darkness in his heart in lines 50–51.

## Scene 5

**BEFORE LINE 1, STAGE DIRECTION.** *As you picture Lady Macbeth reading this letter, try to imagine what she would be doing onstage and what her mood would be, especially at the words "Thane of Cawdor."*

ANSWER. Encourage students to discuss movement, pauses, and reactions. She might be pacing, reading lines with varying emphasis, laughing at some points, and frowning at others.

**LINE 17.** *What might Lady Macbeth do with the letter? Whom is she addressing here with "thou" and "thy" (lines 14–15)? How would you explain "th' milk of human kindness"?*

ANSWER. Lady Macbeth might clutch the letter to her breast or tuck it into her dress. She is addressing the absent Macbeth. Students may associate the phrase with caring or sensitive human feelings, possibly associated with the tenderness of a mother nursing her infant.

**LINE 27.** *What do you guess the "golden round" is?*

ANSWER. It is the king's crown.

**LINE 37.** *Who is the raven she refers to as being hoarse? Why does she call him a raven?*

ANSWER. She may be speaking figuratively of the raven as a symbol of evil, or she may be referring to the messenger as bringing news that bodes ill for Duncan.

**LINE 53.** *How has Lady Macbeth reinforced the witches' statement "Fair is foul, and foul is fair"?*

ANSWER. She has prayed that her finest qualities be turned to foulness.

**LINE 58.** *Is the Macbeths' passion for each other as great as their passion for power? If you feel it is, how might a director illustrate it here?*

ANSWER. Students may say that Macbeth's greeting suggests real passion. A director might have Macbeth and Lady Macbeth embrace or gaze into each other's eyes.

**LINE 70.** *How is Macbeth feeling?*

ANSWER. He might be impressed by his wife's fervor; he might be eager to pursue the enterprise; he might be desiring assurance that all will be well.

## Scene 6

**LINE 9.** *This scene contrasts strongly with the previous one. What irony does the audience feel as Duncan admires the castle? How do you imagine Lady Macbeth acts as she enters to greet her guests?*

ANSWER. The audience feels dramatic irony—while the audience knows that evil lurks within (the Macbeths plan to kill Duncan), the visitors remark on how pleasant the place is; this is an illustration of the adage "Fair is foul and foul is fair." Lady Macbeth probably pretends to be pleased and flattered by the royal visit.

**LINE 31.** *How do you imagine the scene ends?*

ANSWER. Perhaps Duncan and Lady Macbeth join hands and move together offstage, or perhaps the king graciously kisses her hand.

## Scene 7

**LINE 1.** *This is one of Shakespeare's great soliloquies, in which Macbeth voices his indecision and possibly his misgivings. What conflicts is he experiencing?*

ANSWER. He is afraid of the consequences of the murder. He has obligations as Duncan's kinsman, subject, and host. He is afraid that Duncan's death might outrage people. He is motivated by ambition, not by hatred of Duncan or disgust with his actions as king.

**LINE 25.** *Macbeth says, "I have no spur / To prick the sides of my intent. . . ." Is that true?*

ANSWER. Students may say yes: Without ambition there is no reason for Macbeth to kill Duncan. Or they may say no: Lady Macbeth provides a spur.

*Drama Study Guide: **The Tragedy of Macbeth***

**LINE 54.** *How does Lady Macbeth try to intimidate her husband in this speech? Notice what she says about herself in the next few lines. There has been some doubt about whether "We fail?" (line 59) should be a question. How does the meaning change if the line is spoken as a statement?*

**ANSWER.** She challenges Macbeth's manliness and makes murder seem easy. Students may argue that the statement could be meant ironically, unbelievingly, or mockingly.

**LINE 72.** *"Quell" is murder. What are Lady Macbeth's plans?*

**ANSWER.** She plans to get Duncan's chamberlains so drunk that they pass out; she and Macbeth will murder Duncan and frame the servants.

**LINE 81.** *Should the actor playing Macbeth pause here? How should these key words be spoken?*

**ANSWER.** The actor might pause. The tone might be grim or sad yet defiant.

**LINE 82.** *How is this yet another echo of the witches' words in Scene 1?*

**ANSWER.** The mask of a fair face conceals the foul heart.

---

# Act II Scene 1

**BEFORE LINE 1, STAGE DIRECTION.** *Who is Fleance? What do you remember of the witches' prophecy when you see him here? Do we know whether Macbeth and his wife have any children?*

**ANSWER.** Fleance is Banquo's son. Earlier the witches told Banquo, "Thou shalt get kings, though thou be none" (Act I, Scene 3, line 67). The play contains no information about the Macbeths' having children other than Lady Macbeth's reference to having nursed a baby.

**LINE 24.** *This is the second time Macbeth has suggested that he and Banquo talk. Do you think he might want to confide in Banquo? Does he want to get Banquo on his side? How would you characterize his motives?*

**ANSWER.** He may wish to persuade Banquo to side with him, or he may want to find out what Banquo is thinking. Because Macbeth uses veiled speech, it is not clear whether he is trying to find out whether Banquo would support his claim if Duncan died naturally or whether he is trying to make Banquo an accessory to the crime. Students may say his motives are self-serving.

**LINE 32.** *What is the ringing of the bell to mean?*

**ANSWER.** The bell is to signal the murder of Duncan.

**LINE 41.** *What does Macbeth do at this moment? If you were directing the play, would you suspend a dagger in front of Macbeth during this speech? Why or why not?*

**ANSWER.** He draws his own dagger to compare it with the imaginary one. Some students may say that an imaginary dagger is more effective; others, that an actual dagger would emphasize the power of his imagination.

**LINE 64.** *Trace a vision, a call to action, and a leave-taking in this soliloquy. What should you be feeling as a member of the audience when Macbeth exits?*

**ANSWER.** A vision is evoked in lines 33–47; a call to action, in line 62; leave-taking, in lines 63–64. Students may suggest horror, revulsion, or suspense.

## Scene 2

**LINE 3.** *What sound would you hear here? In this soliloquy, who does "them" refer to? Who is "He"?*

**ANSWER.** The audience would hear an owl shrieking. The grooms are "them"; Macbeth is "He."

**LINE 13.** *How should Lady Macbeth say this last line, which reveals why the plans have changed? Do you think she is beginning to show remorse?*

**ANSWER.** She might speak with tenderness, with surprise at her own inability to overcome her emotions, or with remorse. If she is not feeling remorse, she at least shows a more vulnerable side of her character.

**LINE 33.** *Is Lady Macbeth fighting for control here?*

**ANSWER.** Students may say that she is, that "must not" and "make us mad" suggest she is also

*Drama Study Guide: **The Tragedy of Macbeth***

troubled. Or they may say that she is trying to calm Macbeth.

**LINE 41.** *Who else has complained about sleep? In what way has Macbeth "murdered sleep"?*

**ANSWER.** Banquo decided not to sleep in order to avoid evil dreams (Act II, Scene 1). Since first imagining Duncan's murder, Macbeth has been stuck in time at the moment of the murder. Now, without sleep to make the transition to a new day, it seems as if he may continue to relive the moment. So for Macbeth the murder of Duncan has put an end to sleep and may have put an end to the passage of time.

**LINE 46.** *What is the "filthy witness"? What actions are the couple engaged in here? In the next line, Lady Macbeth discovers the daggers. Why is she so alarmed at seeing them in her husband's hands? How might Macbeth have been carrying them so that they weren't visible before?*

**ANSWER.** The "filthy witness" is Duncan's blood. They are cleaning up after the murder. Lady Macbeth is probably shocked that Macbeth has removed the murder weapons; being seen with them would implicate him, and his action shows a lack of attention on his part that she may find frightening. Earlier they might have been in his belt or sleeve.

**LINE 55.** *What will Lady Macbeth do to the grooms if Duncan bleeds enough?*

**ANSWER.** She will smear Duncan's blood on their faces.

**LINE 63.** *On the basis of this speech, how do you think Lady Macbeth looks?*

**ANSWER.** Students may say that her hands are bloody—from the daggers and from smearing the grooms with blood—but she appears confident.

**LINE 71.** *How is Macbeth acting?*

**ANSWER.** He is lost in thought.

**FOLLOWING LINE 72, STAGE DIRECTION.** *In the theater this sharp, loud knocking is frightening. In the next line, what might Macbeth wish the knocking could do for him?*

**ANSWER.** Students may say that he might wish it could awake him from sleep to find that he had not killed Duncan so that he could escape the horror he now feels.

# Scene 3

**BEFORE LINE 1, STAGE DIRECTION.** *Note that the porter is drunk. What would he be doing during this long speech while the knocking persists?*

**ANSWER.** He might stagger, fumble with the gates or keys, pantomime the people he is imagining, put his hands over his ears, pretend to do his own knocking, or forget what he is doing.

**LINE 36.** *All the time this humorous bantering is going on, what do we know the king's men are about to discover?*

**ANSWER.** They will soon find the body of Duncan and the bloodied grooms.

**LINE 51.** *How must Macbeth be feeling?*

**ANSWER.** That he changes his statement suggests that he is nervous and unsure of himself.

**LINE 58.** *In Elizabethan times many people believed that nature mirrored terrible things happening to human beings, especially to kings. How does this weather mirror what was happening to the king in Macbeth's castle?*

**ANSWER.** Unnatural winds and voices, screeching owls, and earthquakes parallel the unnatural death of Duncan.

**LINE 59.** *A single line, but full of irony—how would Macbeth say it?*

**ANSWER.** The line is ironic because the night was rough for reasons that Macbeth knows but Lennox does not know. Macbeth would probably try to sound natural as he carries on his part of the conversation.

**LINE 67.** *How would you explain Macduff's metaphors?*

**ANSWER.** Macduff speaks of the king as a sacred building that it is a sacrilege to attack. His image suggests the concept of kings as divinely anointed.

**LINE 86.** *The emphasis on Lady Macbeth's gentleness and fairness when we know the foulness underneath might well provoke a snicker from the audience. The snicker might be expected to grow into a laugh when she says, "What, in our house?" These are difficult moments to act. How do you think Lady Macbeth should be behaving?*

*Drama Study Guide: **The Tragedy of Macbeth***

**ANSWER.** Students may say that she should play the part seriously, expressing the surprise and horror that such a deed merits.

**❓ LINE 98.** *Macbeth and Lady Macbeth might well look at each other at this moment. In the next speech, does Lennox draw the conclusion*

*they wanted him to draw—that the servants killed Duncan?*

**ANSWER.** Some students may say that "as it seemed" suggests that Lennox is not fully convinced. Others may argue that when Lennox says "No man's life was to be trusted with them," this is as good as an indictment.

---

# Act III  Scene 1

**❓ LINE 10.** *How would you describe Banquo's mood? Is he envious, or is he thoughtful and troubled?*

**ANSWER.** Banquo is thoughtful and troubled; he suspects that Macbeth has helped the prophecies along and wonders about the prophecies about him and his descendants.

**❓ LINE 35.** *Macbeth has asked three important questions in this scene. What are they? How do you think he would ask them?*

**ANSWER.** Macbeth asks whether Banquo is going riding, how far he is going, and whether Fleance will accompany him. He would probably try to speak casually.

**❓ LINE 42.** *Notice that Macbeth uses the "royal we"; that is, he speaks of himself as "we," as a representative of all the people. Why does he want to be alone?*

**ANSWER.** Students may realize that he wants the others to think that he will be alone because, as soon becomes obvious, he is involved in another evil deed.

**❓ LINE 63.** *What is an "unlineal hand"? What is a "barren scepter" (line 62)? What is eating at Macbeth now?*

**ANSWER.** Both terms refer to the idea of a king without offspring. Macbeth is upset that Banquo's sons will inherit Macbeth's throne.

**❓ LINE 72.** *Why is Macbeth so angry? What has he given up in order to make Banquo's sons kings?*

**ANSWER.** He is angry because he has endangered his own soul by committing the foul sin of murder so that another man's sons can become kings. He has given up the chance that after his death his would go to heaven.

**❓ LINE 74.** *What do you imagine the murderers would be like? Would they be the hit men of contemporary movies or simply officers who have a grudge against Banquo? (They have been portrayed in many ways.)*

**ANSWER.** After students have read the scene, return to this question. They may suggest that the murderers are solid citizens who support Macbeth.

**❓ LINE 91.** *What technique is Macbeth using on the murderers? Does it remind you of the way Lady Macbeth goaded him into killing Duncan?*

**ANSWER.** Macbeth is convincing the murderers that Banquo is to blame for their troubles. He attacks their manhood as Lady Macbeth attacked his.

**❓ LINE 126.** *How does Macbeth justify to the murderers the fact that he has to ask them to do the job of killing Banquo?*

**ANSWER.** Macbeth argues that he must appear unblemished in order to retain, for political reasons, the goodwill of friends of his and Banquo's.

**❓ LINE 140.** *What has Macbeth arranged with the murderers? What is his mood here? Does Lady Macbeth have any part in arranging these next murders?*

**ANSWER.** Macbeth has arranged to give them instructions for carrying out the murders. He is calculating, controlled. Lady Macbeth has no part in the arrangements.

## Scene 2

**❓ LINE 7.** *What reversal of attitudes is taking place here?*

**ANSWER.** Finding that she and Macbeth must now live with fear and suspicion, Lady Macbeth is beginning to believe that the throne is not worth the price of their evil deeds.

---

*Drama Study Guide: **The Tragedy of Macbeth***

**LINE 12.** *This scene can be played in several ways. Is Lady Macbeth hostile to and angry with her husband? Or does she display any tenderness in this scene?*

**ANSWER.** She may be sympathetic, pleading, cajoling, or scolding.

**LINE 26.** *What do you picture the couple doing in this scene? Are they sitting together? Are they close, or is there a distance between them?*

**ANSWER.** Students who see the Macbeths as still emotionally close or dependent may say that they will touch each other as one or the other moves about. Students who note that Lady Macbeth complains that her husband keeps to himself may say that they are drifting apart and that they will avoid touching.

**LINE 35.** *With what degree of urgency should Lady Macbeth say this line?*

**ANSWER.** Lady Macbeth should speak with great urgency and fear. She is worried about Macbeth's state of mind.

## Scene 3

**LINE 1.** *The identity of the Third Murderer is not made clear. Whom would you name as possible suspects?*

**ANSWER.** He may be a messenger sent by Macbeth, Macbeth himself, or one of Macbeth's officers.

**LINE 17.** *What are the murderers doing as the light goes out (see line 19)?*

**ANSWER.** They are attacking Banquo.

**LINE 22.** *Disposal of bodies is always a problem for directors of Shakespeare's plays. How would you have Banquo's body carried off? By whom?*

**ANSWER.** Since Shakespeare's plays were written for a theater in the round and curtains could not be drawn, one possibility would be to have the murderers move the body.

**LINE 22.** *This scene, so crucial to the play, is often called the play's turning point or technical climax. What victories has Macbeth won so far?*

**ANSWER.** He has acquired Cawdor and the throne, and although he has aroused suspicion, he is apparently without open opposition. Fleance's escape is his first setback.

## Scene 4

**LINE 2.** *This crucial scene is often called the dramatic climax of the play; it is tremendously exciting when staged well. As you read through it, note the point at which Macbeth's subjects become aware of his capacity for irrational behavior.*

**ANSWER.** Students should recognize that the subjects become wary around lines 48–52.

**LINE 20.** *How would Macbeth react to this line?*

**ANSWER.** He might be surprised, horrified, or angry.

**LINE 37.** *Lady Macbeth has summoned her husband to her area of the stage. What mood is she in?*

**ANSWER.** She may be alarmed, concerned, or irritated.

**WHITHIN LINE 37, STAGE DIRECTION.** *The ghost is crucial to this scene. From what you read here, do you think the ghost should be imagined? Or should it appear onstage? If it does appear, how should it look?*

**ANSWER.** A good case can be made for either an imagined ghost or a ghost played by the actor who plays Banquo. The ghost should appear with gashes on his head or throat.

**LINE 46.** *When Macbeth says this line, what does he see?*

**ANSWER.** He sees Banquo's ghost occupying his own seat.

**LINE 49.** *How should Macbeth ask this question? Whom should he be talking to?*

**ANSWER.** He should be angry or horrified; he is accusing his guests of playing a cruel joke on him.

**LINE 51.** *According to Macbeth's speech here, what is the ghost doing? Does anyone else see the ghost? How should the guests be acting?*

**ANSWER.** The ghost is shaking its head at him. No one else sees the ghost. The guests should act surprised, embarrassed, alarmed, or frightened by Macbeth's behavior.

**LINE 53.** *Do you think this is true? Or is Lady Macbeth desperately trying to cover for her husband?*

**ANSWER.** Even though Macbeth previously imagined a dagger, no specific illness has been mentioned. She is covering for him.

*Drama Study Guide: The Tragedy of Macbeth*

**44**    HRW MATERIAL COPYRIGHTED UNDER NOTICE APPEARING EARLIER IN THIS WORK.

**LINE 58.** *Where do you think Lady Macbeth has taken her husband so that she can whisper this intimidating line?*

**ANSWER.** She has pulled him away from the guests.

**LINE 68.** *What could the actor playing the ghost do here in mockery of Macbeth?*

**ANSWER.** He could stare in a frightening way at Macbeth, shake his head, and make threatening gestures.

**LINE 70.** *What is Macbeth doing here? What is his tone?*

**ANSWER.** He is pointing to the ghost and perhaps turning to Lady Macbeth for confirmation of what he sees. Perhaps he speaks in a despairing tone or in a mocking manner.

**LINE 75.** *Whom is Macbeth talking to?*

**ANSWER.** He seems to be talking to himself. He is clearly not talking to the ghost, who has exited.

**LINE 85.** *What impression is Macbeth trying to create?*

**ANSWER.** Following Lady Macbeth's lead, he is trying to create the impression that he is a calm host, making apologies for his behavior. Notice his strength in lines 84–92 as he, at least momentarily, dismisses the frightening vision of Banquo's ghost.

**LINE 93.** *Whom is Macbeth talking to now? According to this speech, what is the ghost doing?*

**ANSWER.** He is talking to Banquo's ghost, who stares accusingly at him.

**LINE 108.** *How brave does Macbeth appear to be, given all the "brave" talk in these lines? What is he feeling when he says "I am a man again"?*

**ANSWER.** He is brave enough to plant his feet firmly on the floor though he is shaking and terrified. He is feeling relief.

**LINE 110.** *Lady Macbeth and her husband converse in private again. What might the guests be doing?*

**ANSWER.** They might be speaking in subdued whispers or glancing or gesturing toward Macbeth.

**LINE 117.** *What clue here might tell the actor playing Macbeth how he is to behave?*

**ANSWER.** "He grows worse and worse" suggests that he may be staring or babbling; he is oblivious of his guests.

**LINE 122.** *Read this speech carefully, and decide how Macbeth would deliver it: slow? fast? What is his mood?*

**ANSWER.** The speech is often spoken slowly in a weary, resigned manner.

**LINE 127.** *Is the old fire still present in Lady Macbeth? Or is she suddenly tired and broken?*

**ANSWER.** Lady Macbeth is exhausted; her fire is spent.

**LINE 140.** *Does the prospect of a new adventure animate Macbeth? Or is he spent and exhausted?*

**ANSWER.** Students who think he is spent and exhausted may cite the word *tedious* or the lines in which Lady Macbeth points out that he is exhausted because he lacks sleep. Others may say that lines 139–140 and 143–144 suggest that he is ready to move on and immerse himself further in evil.

**LINE 144.** *How might Lady Macbeth react to this last line?*

**ANSWER.** She might shake her head in sorrow and dismay.

## Scene 5

**LINE 1.** Macbeth *was published in the first folio in 1623, seven years after Shakespeare died. Some people think that this scene was written by someone else because the play was short and needed fleshing out. After you read the scene, decide whether you think it "sounds" like the rest of the play.*

**ANSWER.** The lines here differ markedly from the blank verse (unrhymed iambic pentameter) of most of the play. From line 2 on, the scene is written in rhymed couplets.

## Scene 6

**LINE 24.** *Lennox is sometimes called the ironic character of the play. Do you agree? What tone would he use in this speech?*

**ANSWER.** Lennox has spoken with some irony or doubt in his voice on previous occasions, as in reporting the blood-smeared grooms (Act II, Scene

*Drama Study Guide: **The Tragedy of Macbeth***

HRW MATERIAL COPYRIGHTED UNDER NOTICE APPEARING EARLIER IN THIS WORK.

**45**

3, lines 100–103). The irony in these lines comes through most clearly when they are read aloud. Read the speech aloud to the class, or coach a student to read it to express the irony.

**?** **LINE 49.** *This is basically an "information" scene. Summarize what it tells you about the plot.*

**ANSWER.** The lords have grown so suspicious about Duncan's death, Macbeth's motive for silencing the grooms, and his placing blame on those who have fled that Malcolm and Macduff are working in England to raise an army against Macbeth.

---

# Act IV   Scene 1

**?** **BEFORE LINE 1, STAGE DIRECTION.** *This scene usually begins in darkness. In Shakespeare's day the caldron might have risen through the trapdoor. How would you have the witches act: gleeful? lamenting?*

**ANSWER.** The witches might be gleeful or engrossed.

**?** **LINE 1.** *This exciting scene has five major sections, each with its own intensity. See whether you can identify them after you've finished reading the scene.*

**ANSWER.** Possible divisions are (1) the caldron scene, (2) Hecate's and Macbeth's appearances, (3) the three apparitions, (4) the show of eight kings, and (5) Macbeth's talk with Lennox.

**?** **LINE 49.** *How has Macbeth's attitude toward the witches changed since his earlier encounters with them?*

**ANSWER.** He is no longer awed by them. Totally contemptuous, he treats them with disrespect.

**?** **LINE 61.** *This exchange is spoken rapidly. Do the witches now see Macbeth as a participant in evil?*

**ANSWER.** Students who recall Hecate's lines in Act III, Scene 5, may say that Macbeth is not a full participant in evil. Students who focus on this scene may say that the witches identify him as an evil person now.

**?** **LINE 68.** *What are the witches doing throughout this scene?*

**ANSWER.** Students may say that they are tossing ingredients into the caldron and muttering while speaking with Macbeth.

**?** **LINE 71.** *Why does the helmeted head deliver this message? How does the form of the apparition support the warning it gives?*

**ANSWER.** Perhaps the helmeted head delivers this message in order to warn Macbeth that Macduff could defeat him. The helmet suggests that such a defeat might take place in battle.

**?** **LINE 82.** *Macbeth takes the child's message to mean that he need not fear Macduff. Nonetheless, why should the second apparition's message be approached with caution?*

**ANSWER.** At first the message seems to mean that no one can harm Macbeth, but the wording is unusual and may be a riddle.

**?** **LINE 94.** *What does the third apparition prophesy? What must Macbeth's mental state be at this point?*

**ANSWER.** The apparition prophesies that Macbeth (in his castle at Dunsinane) will not be defeated until Birnam Wood marches on Dunsinane. He must feel exultant, unbeatable, since the second and third prophecies seem to go against reason.

**?** **LINE 103.** *What is Macbeth's mood? How might his tone change when he asks about Banquo's issue, or children?*

**ANSWER.** Macbeth is consumed by the desire to know whether Banquo's descendants will inherit his throne. His tone might change from exultation to concern.

**?** **FOLLOWING LINE 111, STAGE DIRECTION.** *A parade of eight Stuart kings passes before Macbeth. These are the kings of Banquo's line. The last king holds up a glass (a mirror) to suggest an endless line of descendants. Banquo appears last. According to the next speech, how does Banquo act toward Macbeth?*

**ANSWER.** He smiles at Macbeth and gestures to indicate that the eight kings are his descendants.

**?** **LINE 124.** *How does Banquo look? What must Macbeth's mental state be now?*

*Drama Study Guide: The Tragedy of Macbeth*

**46**

HRW MATERIAL COPYRIGHTED UNDER NOTICE APPEARING EARLIER IN THIS WORK.

**ANSWER.** Banquo still has bloody gashes. Macbeth must be angry and dismayed that despite the three promising prophecies, Banquo will win in the end.

**? LINE 135.** *How would the mood onstage change as Lennox appears?*

**ANSWER.** Lennox's appearance marks the sudden return of everyday reality and sanity, or perhaps it redirects the audience's attention to the suspense surrounding the thanes' increasing suspicions and Macduff's attempts to raise an army against Macbeth.

**? LINE 142.** *What crucial information does Lennox give Macbeth?*

**ANSWER.** Lennox tells Macbeth that Macduff has fled to England.

**? LINE 156.** *In this speech, how does Macbeth show he has fallen ever deeper into evil? How different is Macbeth now from the reluctant murderer of the first part of the play? Why does he want to murder Macduff's children?*

**ANSWER.** Whereas Macbeth earlier was indecisive and had to work himself up to kill Duncan, now he has grown so evil that he can order murder without a second thought. Students may say that the difference between a reluctant murderer and a habitual murderer is small compared with the difference between an innocent man and a reluctant murderer. They may say that Macbeth has a good idea of Macduff's intentions, so he may want to murder the children because he hates Macduff.

## Scene 2

**? BEFORE LINE 1, STAGE DIRECTION.** *In many productions the mood of this scene contrasts dramatically with the previous scenes of horror. How would you stage this domestic scene to suggest the vulnerability of Lady Macduff and her children?*

**ANSWER.** The staging should show Lady Macduff's motherly tenderness in stark contrast to Lady Macbeth's coldheartedness and Macbeth's heartlessness.

**? LINE 17.** *How could Ross show his fear?*

**ANSWER.** He might extend his hands as if pleading. He might lower his voice or look over his shoulder.

**? LINE 30.** *In taking his leave, how might Ross show affection for Lady Macduff and her young son?*

**ANSWER.** He might kiss Lady Macduff's cheek and tousle the boy's hair.

**? LINE 31.** *How would you have Lady Macduff act in this scene? frightened? bitter? loving? resigned?*

**ANSWER.** She might act concerned about her husband's absence and about the danger, or she might conceal her fear behind banter with her son.

**? LINE 72.** *Some readers think that this messenger has been sent by Lady Macbeth. Is there any support for this theory? Would it be within her character?*

**ANSWER.** There is no support for the theory because Lady Macbeth does not know of her husband's plans. Furthermore, such an action does not seem to be within her character: Though she may be uncomfortable with the course of events, she has done nothing to try to atone for her and her husband's evil deeds.

**? LINE 78.** *How does Lady Macduff act when she hears this terrible message?*

**ANSWER.** Lady Macduff is unbelieving; she panics; she looks for some way to flee.

**? LINE 84.** *What might Lady Macduff and her son do as they see the murderers enter the room?*

**ANSWER.** The lines that follow suggest that the boy tries to protect his mother—perhaps stepping in front of her to shield her. Perhaps she tries to shield him. Perhaps they both back away.

## Scene 3

**? LINE 14.** *What great irony would the audience feel upon hearing this line, given what has taken place in the previous scene?*

**ANSWER.** Although the audience knows it, neither Malcolm nor Macduff knows that Macbeth has already had Macduff's family killed.

**? LINE 37.** *This speech might present a problem for the actor playing Macduff because it does not clearly relate to what has gone before. It seems too grand and philosophical at this point in the play. How would you have the actor deliver the speech?*

**ANSWER.** He may play it as if disheartened, resigned, offended, insulted, and angry.

*Drama Study Guide:* **The Tragedy of Macbeth**

HRW MATERIAL COPYRIGHTED UNDER NOTICE APPEARING EARLIER IN THIS WORK.

**47**

**LINE 57.** *How has Macduff responded to Malcolm's speech?*

**ANSWER.** Macduff says that no one, not even a devil from hell, is worse than Macbeth.

**LINE 66.** *Why do you think Malcolm is drawing attention to his vices? What could he hope to accomplish?*

**ANSWER.** Ask this question after students have read through line 139. By discussing his imaginary vices, Malcolm can see what Macduff will tolerate. Malcolm seems to be testing Macduff to see how sincere he is about wanting Malcolm to depose Macbeth. Malcolm may also be trying to determine where Macduff's loyalty lies.

**LINE 84.** *How do you imagine Malcolm delivers this speech? How could his delivery affect Macduff's response?*

**ANSWER.** Ask this question after students have read through line 139. Malcolm must convince Macduff yet let the audience know that all these allegations about him are false. An ironic delivery would indicate that Malcolm is teasing and might elicit a jesting tone from Macduff; a serious delivery might elicit a more concerned response from Macduff.

**LINE 114.** *How might Malcolm's tone change here? How has Macduff proved himself?*

**ANSWER.** Malcolm drops his sinful, man-of-the-world air and speaks in his normal, gentle tone. Macduff has shown that he is totally loyal to Scotland and is repulsed by such crimes as those committed by Macbeth.

**LINE 137.** *Where should Malcolm pause in this line? Should he act puzzled or matter-of-fact?*

**ANSWER.** There should be a fairly sharp break before "Why are you silent?" Most students will think that Malcolm is probably matter-of-fact and aware that he has stunned Macduff.

**WITHIN LINE 159, STAGE DIRECTION.** *Ross is Macduff's countryman. What news do you anticipate he brings with him?*

**ANSWER.** Students may say that Ross brings an update on Macbeth, or they may guess that he brings the news that Macduff's family has been murdered.

**LINE 176.** *Does Ross look at Macduff on this line, or does he turn away?*

**ANSWER.** He probably looks away, all too aware of "the newest grief" he must report.

**LINE 179.** *What is the double meaning of this line?*

**ANSWER.** For Macduff, "peace" means that his family is well. For Ross it means the peace that comes in death.

**LINE 203.** *Macduff's pain becomes visible. How should we see it?*

**ANSWER.** We should probably see it in his face and hear it in his tone of voice—he seems to have guessed at least part of the truth from Ross's hedging.

**LINE 211.** *How full, or soft, a voice would you have Macduff use in this line?*

**ANSWER.** Macduff might whisper or cry out in distress or try to master his feelings and attempt to speak in a controlled, normal tone.

**LINE 216.** *How would Macduff say "He has no children"?*

**ANSWER.** If students think Macduff refers to Macbeth, they might think he speaks with pain and scorn. If he speaks of Malcolm, he might seem to be reminding himself that there are reasons for Malcolm's lack of understanding, and his voice and tone might be less harsh, even sad.

**LINE 220.** *Is Malcolm being critical or encouraging here?*

**ANSWER.** Malcolm is urging Macduff to act on his feelings. Malcolm's desire to grieve for his father at the beginning of the scene suggests that he would not criticize Macduff for showing his feelings.

# Act V   Scene 1

**LINE 22.** *Why must Lady Macbeth have light by her continually?*

**ANSWER.** She is afraid of the dark, perhaps associating it with murder or hell, which in line 35 she calls "murky," meaning "dark and gloomy."

**LINE 30.** *What is Lady Macbeth doing with her hands?*

**ANSWER.** Having found an invisible spot of blood, she is trying to wash it out.

**? LINE 39.** *What does she think is on her hands?*

**ANSWER.** She thinks Duncan's blood is on her hands.

**? LINE 41.** *Who is the Thane of Fife?*

**ANSWER.** Macduff is the Thane of Fife.

**? LINE 49.** *What action is suggested by this line?*

**ANSWER.** Lady Macbeth is sniffing at an imaginary spot on one hand.

**? LINE 62.** *Whom does she think she is speaking to here?*

**ANSWER.** She thinks she is speaking to Macbeth.

**? LINE 66.** *Once again there is a dramatic change. What echo from the past brings it about? How do you think Lady Macbeth leaves the stage?*

**ANSWER.** She thinks she hears knocking at the gate, as in Act II, Scene 2. She leaves the stage in frantic haste.

**? LINE 77.** *What does the doctor know? Why won't he speak out?*

**ANSWER.** He recognizes the truth about Duncan's murder but realizes that speaking out would endanger his life.

## Scene 2

**? LINE 5.** *Where have you heard about Birnam Wood before?*

**ANSWER.** The third apparition (Act IV, Scene 1, lines 92–94) said, "Macbeth shall never vanquished be until / Great Birnam Wood to high Dunsinane Hill / Shall come against him."

**? LINE 31.** *The "falling action" of a play by Shakespeare is usually swift. How does this scene show that the hero's enemies are now rallying to crush him? What group is shown in this scene?*

**ANSWER.** The thanes of Scotland (those present) now openly oppose Macbeth and are marching toward Dunsinane. They report that English forces, along with Malcolm and Macduff, are on the way to join them.

## Scene 3

**? LINE 12.** *Macbeth is in an extreme state of agitation. Which of the apparitions' prophecies is he relying on?*

**ANSWER.** He is relying on the prophecies that he cannot be defeated until Birnam Wood comes to Dunsinane and that "no man . . . born of woman" can defeat him.

**? LINE 18.** *How would you stage Macbeth's treatment of the servant?*

**ANSWER.** He treats the servant scornfully, standing proud and impatiently finishing the servant's sentences while the servant perhaps cowers in fear.

**? LINE 22.** *What mood is Macbeth in now?*

**ANSWER.** Students may be confused by the contradiction between line 21, in which Macbeth seems to think there is a possibility of success, and line 22, in which he sounds defeated and resigned.

**? LINE 37.** *Who is the doctor's patient?*

**ANSWER.** It is Lady Macbeth.

**? LINE 56.** *This speech contains almost a roller coaster of emotions. Can you cite some?*

**ANSWER.** Some possibilities are disgust, irritation, self-pity, concern for the country, and whimsy.

**? LINE 60.** *Is Macbeth truly courageous here? Or do you think that he is merely coasting on a kind of false bravery lent him by the witches' prophecies?*

**ANSWER.** He seems to be shoring himself up with bravado based on the enigmatic words of the apparitions.

## Scene 4

**? LINE 5.** *Describe what the soldiers are to do here and why.*

**ANSWER.** Each soldier is to cut a leafy branch and carry it in front of him to use as camouflage.

**? LINE 7.** *Malcolm seems to have more authority at this point in the play. Can you find specific instances where his new authority could be dramatized?*

**ANSWER.** He might lead the troops or give orders; by their manner, others could show that they defer to and protect him.

## Scene 5

**? LINE 7.** *Macbeth's behavior should contrast with Malcolm's now. How should Macbeth be acting?*

*Drama Study Guide: **The Tragedy of Macbeth***

**ANSWER.** In contrast to Malcolm's calm forcefulness, Macbeth might act bitter and scornful and show false bravery.

**? LINE 28.** *A scene that began in defiance changes with this great speech. What is Macbeth's new mood? Does he speak only for himself here or for the general human condition?*

**ANSWER.** Students may say that he shows philosophical resignation to the shortness and meaninglessness of life. Though they may not agree with Macbeth, they should see that he laments the human condition.

**? LINE 35.** *What is Macbeth thinking of now?*

**ANSWER.** He is recalling the prophecy about Birnam Wood's advancing on Dunsinane.

**? LINE 52.** *Macbeth ends the scene in a state of great emotion. How would you characterize his mental state?*

**ANSWER.** Having seen the duplicity of one prophecy, Macbeth experiences the inner fatigue of final despair. Realizing that it matters little whether he remains in the castle or goes out, he resolves to die fighting.

## Scene 7

**? LINE 4.** *What is Macbeth desperately clinging to now?*

**ANSWER.** He is clinging to the prophecy that he interprets as meaning no living person can harm him, since everyone is born of a woman.

## Scene 8

**? LINE 16.** *What is the meaning of lines 15–16? How do they relate to the prophecy?*

**ANSWER.** Macduff was not "of woman born" in the natural way but was delivered by Caesarean section.

**? LINE 53.** *What character traits does Malcolm show in this scene? How is Siward like a military man to the end?*

**ANSWER.** Malcolm exhibits great concern for each missing man and promises some posthumous honor for Young Siward. Like a military man, Siward is satisfied that his son has died bravely and so says that no further honor is necessary.

**? FOLLOWING LINE 53, STAGE DIRECTION.** *Macduff enters with Macbeth's head on a pole. A great shout goes up. What is Macduff's tone in the next speech?*

**ANSWER.** He is relieved, gracious, moved, jubilant.

**? LINE 75.** *Scone (usually pronounced "scoon") is a stone upon which the Scottish kings sat at their coronation. (It is now in Westminster Abbey in London, beneath the coronation chair of the English kings.) How would you have the characters exit? Who would exit last?*

**ANSWER.** Students might suggest that Malcolm should lead the way and that the others should follow in order of rank.

## Graphic Organizer for Active Reading, Act I

### The Criminal Mind

When we first read about Macbeth, he is a hero, a man who would fight to the death for the king. But by the end of Act I, Macbeth has begun to change. His evil side emerges and threatens to overwhelm his good side. Shakespeare introduces this transformation gradually, showing the moral struggle developing in Macbeth's mind. In the diagram below, write events, dialogue, and thoughts that reflect the changes in Macbeth in Act I. Write attributes of his good side in the arm labeled "The Good Macbeth" and attributes of his evil side in the arm labeled "The Evil Macbeth." Where the hands clasp each other, write events, thoughts, or dialogue that are neutral or ambiguous.

**Neutral / Ambiguous**

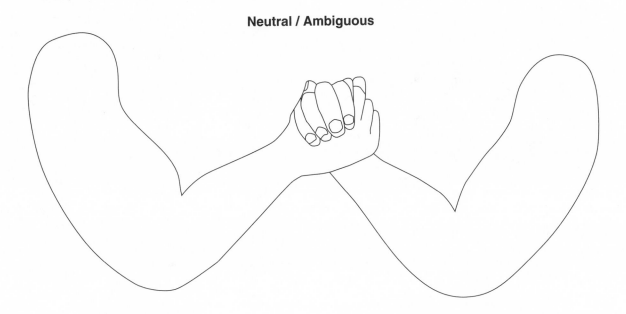

**The Good Macbeth**          **The Evil Macbeth**

1. Do you think Macbeth would have changed if the witches had not appeared? Explain.

   _____

   _____

   _____

2. Do you think most people are as susceptible to temptation as Macbeth? Explain why or why not.

   _____

   _____

   _____

# Making Meanings, Act I

## First Thoughts

1. What are your impressions of Lady Macbeth at the end of Act I? What is her relationship with Macbeth (beyond being his wife)?

## Shaping Interpretations

2. In the very first scene of a play, a dramatist must tell the audience what kind of play they are about to see. What does the brief opening scene of *Macbeth* reveal about the rest of the play? How does the weather reflect the human passions revealed in the rest of the act?

3. How does the witches' prophecy of Macbeth's coming greatness act as a temptation for him?

4. Explain the **paradox,** or the apparently contradictory nature, of the witches' greeting to Banquo in Scene 3: "Lesser than Macbeth, and greater." How is this paradox true?

---

### Reviewing the Text

a. In Scene 1, where do the witches plan to meet again, and why?

b. What news about Macbeth does the bloodstained captain bring to the king in Scene 2?

c. What does the king determine to do for Macbeth? Why?

d. What do the witches tell Macbeth and Banquo in Scene 3?

e. In what lines do you discover Lady Macbeth's plans for Duncan when he visits the castle?

---

5. How does Banquo's reaction to the witches differ from Macbeth's? What do you think Macbeth's reaction suggests about his **character**?

6. One of the most interesting parts of any serious play is what goes on in the characters' minds. What **conflict** rages in Macbeth after he hears the witches' prophecy? What **resolution** to this conflict does Macbeth express in his aside, in Scene 4, lines 48–53?

7. Describe the temperamental differences between Macbeth and his wife. Who is more single-minded and logical? Who is more argumentative and sensitive? Which one wins the argument?

8. What **irony** would the audience feel as they watch Duncan enter the castle and hear him praise its peacefulness?

## Extending the Text

9. One critic has said that the witches are "in some sense representative of potentialities within" Macbeth. How could that statement be explained? Is there any evidence that Macbeth wanted to be king before? Explain your answer.

# Language and Style Mini-Lesson, Act I

## Blank Verse

Almost all of *Macbeth* is written in **blank verse,** or unrhymed iambic pentameter, a form of poetry that comes close to imitating the natural rhythms of English speech. An **iamb** is a metrical foot that has one unstressed syllable followed by one stressed syllable. (Each of the following is an iamb: *Macbeth, success, to win.*) **Pentameter** means that each line of verse has five feet, so one line of iambic pentameter has five iambs:

> **Banquo.** Gŏod sír, wh̆y dó yŏu stárt, ănd seém tŏ feár. . . ?

Some lines in *Macbeth* are irregular, with fewer feet or with feet that are not iambs. The play even has a few prose passages, indicated by lines that are set full measure.

1. Scan one major speech by Macbeth and one by Lady Macbeth anywhere in Act I. What variations in iambic pentameter do you find? Why do you think these variations exist—how do sound and sense relate to each other?

2. Do the witches speak in blank verse? Why do you suppose Shakespeare wrote their speeches in this way?

3. Find a prose passage in Act I. Why do you think Shakespeare chose to use prose in this passage?

## Language Link Worksheet, Act I

### Revision Worksheet

Revise the following essay by correcting all errors in usage, spelling, punctuation, and capitalization. Combine and vary sentences to make the paragraphs read smoothly, and make any other changes that you think will improve the essay. You may substitute or move words and phrases or insert new material.

### The thane of Cawdor: Who Earned the title?

At the conclusion of Act I, Scene 2 of *Macbeth* Duncan decrees the execution of the traitorous Thane of Cawdor then, the next thing, the king directs Ross to "greet Macbeth" with the title. Duncan's decision is ironic because it is Macduff, not Macbeth who deserves the honor.

Ross is closely, throughout the play, identified with macduff. When he reports the events of the war to Duncan in Act I, Scene 2, he says that he comes from Fife, Macduff's castle. Ross announces that the Thane of Cawdor and the Norwegian king, Sweno, have been captured at Fife, Macduff's castle. It is logical to assume therefore that the warrior who Ross refers to as "Bellona's bridegroom" is Macduff. Later, in Act I Scene 3, the witches address Macbeth with the words, "Hail . . . Thane of Cawdor"! Confused, Macbeth rejects the title and describes the Thane of cawdor as "a prosperous gentleman." Macbeth's response prove he no's nothing of the Thane of Cawdor's treachery and being defeated. Indeed, Macbeth deserves to be rewarded by his King. Macbeth did defeat the traitor Macdonwald; beheading him and slitting his body open. It is Macduff, however, who's heroic victories over the Thane of Cawdor and the King of norway is responsible for ending the war. It is both ironic and unjust that having earned the title Macduff does not receive it.

*Drama Study Guide: The Tragedy of Macbeth*

**54**

HRW MATERIAL COPYRIGHTED UNDER NOTICE APPEARING EARLIER IN THIS WORK.

# Literary Elements Worksheet, Act I

## Conflict

**Conflict** is a struggle between opposing characters, forces, or emotions. In an **external conflict** a character struggles against an outside force: another character, society, or nature. In an **internal conflict** opposing needs, desires, or emotions are at odds within a single character.

## Understanding Conflict

As you re-read each passage listed below, decide whether it reflects an internal conflict within Macbeth or an external conflict—either existing or potential. Write the word *internal* or *external* after each of the following numbered passages.

**1.** Scene 3, lines 116–117

_____

**2.** Scene 3, lines 118–120

_____

**3.** Scene 3, lines 139–142

_____

**4.** Scene 3, lines 143–144

_____

**5.** Scene 4, lines 48–50

_____

**6.** Scene 5, lines 61–62

_____

**7.** Scene 7, lines 1–28

_____

**8.** Scene 7, lines 31–45

_____

*(Continued on page 56.)*

*(Continued from page 55.)*

## Applying Skills

Considering the conflicts you identified above, especially the internal conflicts, what do you see as the emerging theme of the play? Give specific reasons for your answer, citing evidence from the text.

_____

_____

_____

_____

_____

_____

### Reader's Response

How do you feel about the relationship between Macbeth and his wife? Describe how the play would be different if Lady Macbeth were a weak, servile character instead of a strong-willed woman. Would Macbeth have committed the murder without his wife's encouragement? Why or why not?

_____

_____

_____

_____

_____

_____

_____

_____

_____

_____

_____

_____

*Drama Study Guide: **The Tragedy of Macbeth***

## Test, Act I

### Thoughtful Reading *(40 points)*

On the line provided, write the letter of the *best* answer to each of the following items. *(8 points each)*

_____ **1.** King Duncan decides to make Macbeth Thane of Cawdor because

    **a.** the last Thane of Cawdor went mad     **c.** the witches told him to
    **b.** Macbeth fought heroically for him     **d.** the last Thane of Cawdor died

_____ **2.** When Macbeth receives his new title, Banquo's reaction is

    **a.** joy     **c.** concern
    **b.** indifference     **d.** jealousy

_____ **3.** After reading the letter from her husband, Lady Macbeth calls upon the spirits to "Make thick my blood, / Stop up th' access and passage to remorse. . . ." She is asking

    **a.** for guidance so that she can maintain her sense of justice and goodness
    **b.** to be made insensitive to the cruelty she is planning
    **c.** for assurance that she and her husband might agree on a plan
    **d.** for access to her husband's unspoken thoughts

_____ **4.** Which of the following quotations from Act I is the *best* example of paradox?

    **a.** "I'll drain him dry as hay. . . ."
    **b.** "Lesser than Macbeth, and greater."
    **c.** "O, never / Shall sun that morrow see!"
    **d.** "Was the hope drunk / Wherein you dressed yourself?"

_____ **5.** Near the end of Act I, Macbeth expresses doubt about murdering the king because

    **a.** Macbeth is the king's subject and host     **c.** the king's sons would kill him
    **b.** it could weaken all of Scotland     **d.** Lady Macbeth has misgivings

### Expanded Response *(30 points)*

**6.** Which of the following quotations *best* describes the mood of Act I? Choose the quotation that accurately communicates the mood. On the lines provided, write the letter of the quotation you choose and briefly defend your choice. There is more than one possible answer. Use at least one example from the selection to support your ideas. *(15 points)*

    **a.** "Fair is foul, and foul is fair."
    **b.** "Come, thick night, / And pall thee in the dunnest smoke of hell. . . ."
    **c.** "False face must hide what the false heart doth know."
    **d.** "The service and the loyalty I owe, / In doing it, pays itself."

_____

_____

_____

_____

_____

*(Continued on page 58.)*

*Drama Study Guide: **The Tragedy of Macbeth***

*(Continued from page 57.)*

**7.** In the left-hand side of the following chart, list character traits that influence Macbeth to become a criminal. In the right-hand side, list events that lead him to commit the crime. *(15 points)*

| Character Traits | External Events |
|---|---|
| | |

# Written Response *(30 points)*

**8.** After a period of indecision, Macbeth confirms his intent to carry out his and Lady Macbeth's plan. On the lines below, write a paragraph describing his thoughts as he makes his decision. What are the reasons for his hesitation? How does he rationalize his choice? Use at least two examples from the play to support your ideas. Use an extra sheet of paper if necessary.

_____

_____

_____

_____

_____

_____

_____

_____

_____

_____

*Drama Study Guide: **The Tragedy of Macbeth***

## Graphic Organizer for Active Reading, Act II

### No Regrets?

Macbeth's character is not purely evil, but in Act II, Macbeth overcomes his reservations long enough to kill King Duncan and two of the king's grooms. Afterward Macbeth reveals his inner state. Search Act II for quotations that disclose Macbeth's feelings about the murders. Write these quotations in the upper, unshaded dagger halves. In the lower, shaded dagger halves, explain each quotation's meaning in your own words.

ACT II

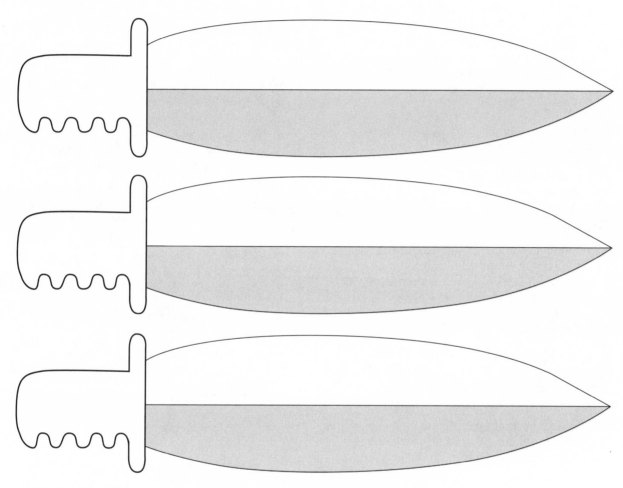

1. Describe Macbeth's general state of mind after the murders.

_____

_____

_____

2. What do you think Macbeth should do to gain control of his feelings?

_____

_____

_____

*Drama Study Guide: **The Tragedy of Macbeth***

# Making Meanings, Act II

## First Thoughts

1. What was your reaction to the murder of Duncan? Why do you think Shakespeare has the murder committed offstage?

## Shaping Interpretations

2. Though Macbeth encounters no opposition until long after Duncan is murdered, Shakespeare **foreshadows** trouble. For there to be **suspense,** one character must start to suspect Macbeth. Who is this, and what hints does he give?

3. In Act I, Lady Macbeth seems to be planning to murder Duncan herself. But in Act II, at the last moment, she is unable to. Consider her reason, and decide what her actions and explanations reveal about her **character.**

4. In Scene 3, Macbeth utters a hypocritical lament beginning "Had I but died." Is it really hypocritical? A critic argued that although the speech is meant to be a lie, it contains "Macbeth's profoundest feelings." Explain this apparent contradiction. How does Macbeth feel about having murdered Duncan? What clues tell you how he feels?

5. Lady Macbeth's fainting spell, like everything else she has done so far, has a purpose. What message do you think she wants her fainting spell to convey?

6. Macduff becomes an important character in the three remaining acts. Describe how Shakespeare **characterizes** him in Scenes 3 and 4.

### Reviewing the Text

a. In Scene 1, Macbeth asks Banquo to meet him later for "some words." What incentive does he offer Banquo? How does Banquo reply?

b. Describe the vision that Macbeth has at the end of Scene 1. What details foreshadow the action to come?

c. In Scene 2, as Macbeth kills Duncan, what does Lady Macbeth hear? What does Macbeth hear?

d. Why, according to Lady Macbeth, was she unable to kill Duncan herself? Which tasks related to the murder does she perform?

e. In Scene 2, how does Macbeth respond to Lady Macbeth's suggestion that he go wash the "filthy witness" from his hands?

f. In Scene 3, what is the porter pretending as he goes to open the gate?

g. Why has Macduff come?

h. What reason does Macbeth give for killing Duncan's two guards?

i. Where do Duncan's sons decide to go?

j. In Scene 4, whom does Macduff suspect of Duncan's murder?

7. What would you say is the **mood** of Act II? What **images** and actions help to create this mood? What do these images **symbolize**?

## Extending the Text

8. How do various characters respond to the violence? How would people today react to the news that a ruler has been assassinated and a nation is in political chaos?

## Challenging the Text

9. In some productions of *Macbeth,* Scene 4 is cut. Why would this be done? Is there any dramatic purpose for keeping it? Why do you think the Old Man is included in the scene?

10. Do you agree with Thomas De Quincey's theories on the knocking at the gate (see the HRW Classics edition of *Macbeth,* pages 132–134)? Why or why not?

*Drama Study Guide: The Tragedy of Macbeth*

# Words to Own Worksheet, Act II

## Developing Vocabulary

Carefully read the definition and explanation of each word and the sample sentence, which shows how the word can be used. Then, write a sentence using the word. In your sentence, include context clues that point to the word's meaning.

1. **augment** (ôg·ment′) *v.* to enlarge; to make greater in size, quantity, or strength. ▲ To *augment* usually implies to increase by addition.

   ■ To augment their living quarters, the Smiths added a room to the back of their house. (Scene 1, line 27)

   Original sentence: _____

   _____

2. **prate** (prāt) *v.* to talk foolishly; to chatter; to blab. ▲ As a noun, *prate* means "idle talk" or "chatter."

   ■ Whenever Simon and Edwin meet, they prate for hours about old times. (Scene 1, line 58)

   Original sentence: _____

   _____

3. **knell** (nel) *n.* the sound of a bell, especially of a bell rung slowly, as at a funeral. ▲ Do not confuse *knell* with *knoll,* meaning "a small, round hill."

   ■ As the mourners gathered at the graveside, they heard the solemn knell of the church bell. (Scene 1, line 63)

   Original sentence: _____

   _____

4. **mad** (mad) *adj.* insane or mentally ill. ▲ *Mad* can also mean "foolish"; "blindly and foolishly enthusiastic"; "wildly amusing"; or "angry."

   ■ Many people think that Solomon is mad, but he is merely eccentric. (Scene 2, line 33)

   Original sentence: _____

   _____

5. **infirm** (in·furm′) *adj.* not firm in mind or purpose. ▲ *Infirm* also means "weak"; "feeble"; "frail"; or "shaky."

   ■ Infirm of purpose, Carmen could not decide which side to support. (Scene 2, line 51)

   Original sentence: _____

   _____

ACT II

*(Continued on page 62.)*

*Drama Study Guide: The Tragedy of Macbeth*

*(Continued from page 61.)*

6. **multitudinous** (mul′tə·tōōd′′n·əs) *adj.* numerous; consisting of many parts or elements. ▲ *Multitudinous,* like *multitude* ("large number") and *multiply* ("to cause to increase in number"), has the Latin root *multus* ("many").

■ Multitudinous wares were sold at the open-air bazaar. (Scene 2, line 61)

Original sentence: _____

_____

7. **rough** (ruf) *adj.* characterized by agitation, disturbance, or irregularity; stormy or tempestuous. ▲ Among several other related meanings of *rough* are "difficult"; "harsh"; "not gentle"; or "lacking comfort or convenience."

■ In rough weather the ferry does not cross the bay. (Scene 3, line 59)

Original sentence: _____

_____

8. **sacrilegious** (sak′rə·lij′əs) *adj.* disrespectful to a person, thing, place, or idea held sacred. ▲ *Sacrilegious* implies treating something religious as if it were secular.

■ The priest proclaimed that the removal of the cross from the church was a sacrilegious, punishable offense. (Scene 3, line 65)

Original sentence: _____

_____

9. **steeped** (stēpt) *adj.* a form of the verb *steep,* which means "to soak in liquid"; "to immerse"; "to saturate." ▲ *Steep* can also mean "to immerse in some kind of knowledge or information," as in "*steep* in culture."

■ The steeped mint leaves made delicious tea. (Scene 3, line 113)

Original sentence: _____

_____

10. **entomb** (en·tōōm′) *v.* to bury or place in a tomb. ▲ The act of burying someone is referred to as *entombment.* Both words derive from the ancient Greek word *tymbos* (a funeral mound).

■ The plan was to entomb the duchess in the cemetery of her ancestors after she died. (Scene 4, line 9)

Original sentence: _____

_____

*Drama Study Guide: **The Tragedy of Macbeth***

# Literary Elements Worksheet, Act II

## Suspense

**Suspense** is the uncertainty or anxiety an audience or a reader feels about what may happen next. A skillful writer builds suspense to keep the reader interested and involved in the plot.

## Understanding Suspense

Answer the following questions about Act II.

1. After Macbeth and Lady Macbeth discussed the possibility of King Duncan's death at the end of Act I, what did you expect to happen at the beginning of Act II?

   _____

   _____

2. How does Macbeth's dagger soliloquy in Scene 1 (up to the sounding of the bell) build suspense?

   _____

   _____

3. What possibility do Lady Macbeth's first two speeches in Scene 2 raise?

   _____

   _____

4. What risk remains after Macbeth has murdered Duncan in Scene 2?

   _____

   _____

5. How does the knocking at the end of Scene 2 help build suspense?

   _____

   _____

6. What is the actual cause of the knocking?

   _____

   _____

7. How does the appearance of the porter in Scene 3 contribute to the suspense?

   _____

   _____

*(Continued on page 64.)*

*Drama Study Guide: **The Tragedy of Macbeth***

**63**

*(Continued from page 63.)*

**8.** What uncertainty remains at the end of Act II?

_____

_____


## Applying Skills

Study the exchange of dialogue in lines 135–146 of Scene 3. How do Malcolm's words foreshadow trouble for Macbeth and build suspense?

_____

_____

_____

_____

_____

_____

_____

*Drama Study Guide: **The Tragedy of Macbeth***

# Test, Act II

## Thoughtful Reading *(40 points)*

On the line provided, write the letter of the *best* answer to each of the following items. *(8 points each)*

_____ **1.** When Macbeth talks agitatedly about the murders, Lady Macbeth urges him to

    **a.** run away immediately     **c.** try not to dwell on them
    **b.** kill the witnesses     **d.** pray for his salvation

_____ **2.** The porter's cursing is ironic because

    **a.** he invokes the devil without knowing about the crime
    **b.** he conveys that nothing is amiss
    **c.** he takes so long to answer the door that Macbeth escapes unnoticed
    **d.** Macbeth does not expect the royal visitors

_____ **3.** When Lennox and Macduff arrive at Macbeth's castle in the morning, their initial impression is that

    **a.** something is terribly wrong
    **b.** everyone has stayed up late and slept in
    **c.** there is a trail of blood around the castle
    **d.** Macbeth is lying to them

_____ **4.** As soon as the murder becomes known, Malcolm and Donalbain flee Scotland because they

    **a.** have lost their inheritance     **c.** believe the country will likely become unstable
    **b.** are guilty of the murder     **d.** suspect someone intends to harm them, too

_____ **5.** The natural disturbances that continue all night—including the screaming owl, chimneys being blown down, and Duncan's horses turning wild—symbolize

    **a.** the inevitable chaos of a terrible storm
    **b.** a coming war with a neighboring country
    **c.** the evil of Macbeth's deeds
    **d.** the imminent flight of the king's sons

## Expanded Response *(30 points)*

**6.** Choose one of the following quotations from Act II. On the lines provided, name the speaker and discuss how the quotation reveals the speaker's character. Use at least one example from the play to support your ideas. *(15 points)*

    **a.** "These deeds must not be thought / After these ways; so, it will make us mad."
    **b.** "Hear [the bell] not, Duncan, for it is a knell / That summons thee to heaven, or to hell."
    **c.** "Why, worthy thane, / You do unbend your noble strength, to think / So brainsickly of things."
    **d.** "O horror, horror, horror! Tongue nor heart / Cannot conceive nor name thee."

_____

_____

_____

_____

*(Continued on page 66.)*

*(Continued from page 65.)*

**7.** Several times, Lady Macbeth tries to ease Macbeth's tormented remorse with comforting remarks. In the diagram below, describe some of these remarks and explain how they help her and Macbeth. *(15 points)*

| Lady Macbeth's Remarks | How the Remarks Help Lady Macbeth and Macbeth |
| --- | --- |
|  |  |

## Written Response *(30 points)*

**8.** On the lines below, write a paragraph describing the mood of Act II. Explain why this mood is appropriate, and discuss why it will likely prevail in the rest of the play. Use at least two examples from Act II to support your ideas. Use an extra sheet of paper if necessary.

_____

_____

_____

_____

_____

_____

_____

_____

_____

_____

*Drama Study Guide: **The Tragedy of Macbeth***

# Graphic Organizer for Active Reading, Act III

## In the Hands of Fate

By Act III, Macbeth has become king, which was his original goal, but his restless mind is getting the better of him. In his soliloquy in Scene 1, Macbeth states a fear that was planted in his mind during his initial encounter with the witches. This fear leads to events that result in Macbeth's seeming madness at his banquet table. In the diagram below, describe the fear, the events, and the banquet scene.

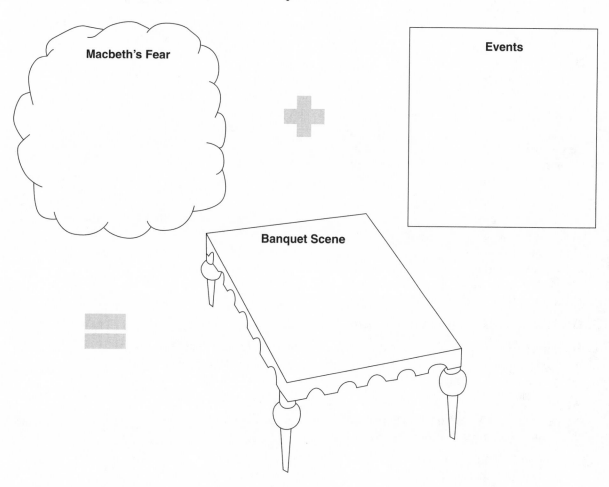

Macbeth's Fear

Events

Banquet Scene

**ACT III**

1. Explain how knowledge of the future has once again driven Macbeth to extreme action.

   _____

   _____

   _____

2. Do you think that Macbeth is foolish to attempt to control what is fated? Or do you think he is acting wisely? Why?

   _____

   _____

   _____

*Drama Study Guide: The Tragedy of Macbeth*

# Making Meanings, Act III

## First Thoughts

1. What title would you give to Act III?

## Shaping Interpretations

2. Why do you suppose Shakespeare did not have Macbeth kill Banquo with his own hands, as he killed Duncan and his two guards? What can you infer about Macbeth's changing **character** after seeing how he engages in this complex plan involving professional murderers?

3. The relationship between Macbeth and Lady Macbeth has changed in several ways since they became rulers of Scotland. Describe some of these changes. What reasons can you suggest for these changes?

4. In Scene 2, Macbeth describes his surroundings by saying, "Light thickens, and the crow / Makes wing to th' rooky wood." How can these remarks also be seen as a **metaphorical** commentary on the events of the play? What other remarks by Macbeth function in this way?

5. How is Fleance's escape a **turning point** in the play?

6. How does the banquet scene blur the clear-cut and common-sense distinction that most of us make between the real and the imaginary? In what other scenes has this distinction also been blurred?

7. At the beginning of Scene 2, Lady Macbeth quietly tells herself, "Nought's had, all's spent, / Where our desire is got without content. . . ." What does she mean? At this point, would her husband agree?

8. Nobody except Macbeth sees Banquo's ghost. In some productions of the play, the ghost does not appear onstage; in others it does. If you were the director, which would you choose? What effect is created by having Banquo appear at the banquet, made up as a ghost? What is gained by having it appear as though no person motivates Macbeth's terrifying behavior?

### Reviewing the Text

a. In the short **soliloquy** that opens Scene 1, what does Banquo reveal about Macbeth? What does he decide to do?

b. How and why does Macbeth arrange Banquo's murder? How is Lady Macbeth involved in the murder?

c. In Scene 3, who escapes the murderers?

d. Describe what happens in Scene 4 when Ross, Lennox, and the other lords invite Macbeth to share their table. What does Macbeth do? What does Lady Macbeth do?

e. Macduff does not appear at all in Act III. Where is he, and why?

f. By Scene 6, what opinion do Lennox and the other lords hold of Macbeth?

## Extending the Text

9. After his vision of Banquo's ghost in Scene 4, Macbeth finally accepts that "blood will have blood." What does this phrase mean? Is it relevant to today's world? How?

## Challenging the Text

10. Shakespeare never reveals the identity of the Third Murderer, introduced in Scene 3. Who do you think the murderer is? Do you think the introduction of this Third Murderer is a flaw in the play? Explain your response.

*Drama Study Guide: **The Tragedy of Macbeth***

**68**

HRW MATERIAL COPYRIGHTED UNDER NOTICE APPEARING EARLIER IN THIS WORK.

## Literary Elements Worksheet, Act III

### Imagery

**Images** are words and phrases that appeal to the reader's senses. Images usually relate directly to the mood, characters, and theme.

### Understanding Imagery

Re-read the following lines and answer the corresponding questions about the images that appear in Act III.

**1.** Scene 1, lines 92–101: To what does Macbeth compare the murderers?

_____

_____

_____

**2.** Scene 2, lines 36–37: What does a mind full of scorpions indicate about Macbeth's mental state?

_____

_____

_____

**3.** Scene 2, lines 50–55: What happens to nature as darkness begins to fall?

_____

_____

_____

**4.** Scene 4, lines 29–31: Whom does Macbeth refer to as a serpent? Who is a worm?

_____

_____

_____

**5.** Scene 4, lines 110–112: How does Macbeth describe his own state of mind?

_____

_____

_____

ACT III

*(Continued on page 70.)*

*Drama Study Guide: **The Tragedy of Macbeth***

**69**

*(Continued from page 69.)*

## Applying Skills

Consider all of the images identified in the previous exercise. What are the main kinds of images that appear in Act III, and what is their overall relation to the play's mood and theme?

_____

_____

_____

_____

_____

_____

_____

_____

_____

_____

_____

_____

_____

_____

_____

_____

_____

_____

_____

_____

_____

_____

_____

_____

_____

*Drama Study Guide: **The Tragedy of Macbeth***

# Test, Act III

## Thoughtful Reading *(40 points)*

On the line provided, write the letter of the *best* answer to each of the following items. *(8 points each)*

_____ **1.** The "barren scepter" Macbeth refers to is a symbol, implying that he

     **a.** will never wield power
     **b.** will have no heirs to the throne
     **c.** will soon be overthrown and slain
     **d.** prefers a smooth scepter barren of decoration

_____ **2.** Macbeth explains to the hired murderers that they must keep his plan a secret because

     **a.** he would be forced to execute them to satisfy the people
     **b.** they would be ostracized for their dirty work
     **c.** he and Banquo have friends in common who would be upset
     **d.** the people should not know about the king's sins

_____ **3.** When Macbeth hears that Fleance has escaped the murderers, he reacts with

     **a.** relief      **b.** anxiety      **c.** happiness      **d.** indifference

_____ **4.** When Macbeth begins talking to Banquo's ghost, Lady Macbeth reacts by

     **a.** telling the others Macbeth has an illness
     **b.** talking loudly so that Macbeth cannot be heard
     **c.** confessing their crimes to the guests
     **d.** pretending she sees the same apparition

_____ **5.** Which of the following phrases is the most vivid example of figurative language in Act III?

     **a.** "As upon thee, Macbeth, their speeches shine. . . ."
     **b.** "O, full of scorpions is my mind, dear wife!"
     **c.** "There's comfort yet; they are assailable."
     **d.** "Blood hath been shed ere now. . . ."

## Expanded Response *(30 points)*

**6.** In the boxes below and on the next page, describe how Macbeth and Lady Macbeth feel about their activities in Acts I, II, and III. On the lines following the diagram, briefly explain why you think both characters change in Act III. *(15 points)*

| Act | Macbeth's Feelings | Lady Macbeth's Feelings |
|-----|--------------------|-------------------------|
| I   |                    |                         |

*(Continued on page 72.)*

*Drama Study Guide: **The Tragedy of Macbeth***

ACT III

*(Continued from page 71.)*

| Act | Macbeth's Feelings | Lady Macbeth's Feelings |
|-----|---------------------|--------------------------|
| II  |                     |                          |

| Act | Macbeth's Feelings | Lady Macbeth's Feelings |
|-----|---------------------|--------------------------|
| III |                     |                          |

_____

_____

_____

_____

7. Which of the following quotations do you think is the most foreboding? On the lines provided, write the letter of the quotation you choose and briefly defend your choice. Each quotation is a valid choice. Use at least one example from the play to support your ideas. *(15 points)*

   **a.** Hecate: "I am for th' air; this night I'll spend / Unto a dismal and a fatal end. . . ."
   **b.** Macbeth: "We are yet but young in deed."
   **c.** Lennox: ". . . that a swift blessing / May soon return to this our suffering country / Under a hand accursed!"
   **d.** Lady Macbeth: "'Tis safer to be that which we destroy / Than by destruction dwell in doubtful joy."

_____

_____

_____

_____

## Written Response *(30 points)*

8. If the ghost of Banquo could speak, what do you think he would say to Macbeth? Would Banquo care enough about his former friend to give him advice, or would he berate Macbeth for murdering him? How do you think Macbeth would react to Banquo's words? On a separate sheet of paper, write an imaginary conversation between Banquo's ghost and Macbeth. Use a combination of dialogue (remember to add quotation marks) and narration.

*Drama Study Guide:* **The Tragedy of Macbeth**

## Graphic Organizer for Active Reading, Act IV

### Evil Is As Evil Does

In Act IV, many characters begin to change allegiances. Most of them can be divided into camps of "good" or "evil" participants in the ongoing moral struggle. Write each name on the appropriate side of the following diagram. Beneath each name, write a brief reason explaining why you believe the character is good or evil. Some boxes may not be used.

|  Macbeth | the Witches | Ross |
|----------|-------------|------|
|  Macduff | Malcolm | the Murderers |

| Good | Evil |
|------|------|
|  |  |
|  |  |
|  |  |
|  |  |

ACT IV

**1.** How do the above allegiances compare with previous allegiances to good and evil?

_____

_____

**2.** Is there any hope that Macbeth can win his former supporters back to his side? Explain.

_____

_____

*Drama Study Guide: **The Tragedy of Macbeth***

# Making Meanings, Act IV

## First Thoughts

1. What effect did the brutal murders of Lady Macduff and her son have on you? Have your feelings for Macbeth changed from the opening of the play until now? How do you account for your reactions?

## Shaping Interpretations

2. In this act, Macbeth seeks out the witches, whereas they initiated the encounter in Act I. How has his situation changed since he last talked with them? How has his moral **character** deteriorated?

3. Do you think the witches have caused any of these changes, directly or indirectly? Explain your reasons for thinking as you do.

4. In Scene 1, the eight kings appear in what was called in Shakespeare's day a **dumb show**—an interpolated brief scene in which nothing is said. What is the point of this particular dumb show?

5. In Scene 2, the lines spoken by Macduff's wife and son illustrate Shakespeare's great skill at **characterization.** Using only a few words, he brings the woman and the child to life. How would you describe Lady Macduff? How would you describe the boy?

6. Both the murderer and Lady Macduff herself call Macduff a traitor. In what sense does each mean it? Do you think Macduff is a traitor in either sense?

7. In Scene 3, Malcolm deliberately lies to Macduff. What does this behavior, and the reason for it, reveal about Malcolm?

### Reviewing the Text

a. What ingredients go into the witches' stew? What symbolic purpose does this vile concoction serve?

b. What has Macbeth come to ask the witches, and how do they answer?

c. Describe the three apparitions Macbeth sees when he visits the witches. What does each apparition tell him?

d. Which nobleman does Macbeth plan to murder after talking with the witches? How is his plan foiled?

e. At the end of Scene 1, what does Macbeth vow? How is his vow carried out in Scene 2?

f. According to the conversation between Malcolm and Macduff in Scene 3, what has happened to Scotland during Macbeth's reign?

g. What faults does Malcolm claim to have?

h. How does Macduff respond to each of Malcolm's three "confessions"?

## Extending the Text

8. In Scene 3, Malcolm and Macduff decry the chaos that Macbeth's rule has brought to Scotland, as if Macbeth's disorder had become Scotland's. Does that happen today—does the weakness or the evil of a nation's leader become that of a nation itself? Explain your response.

## Challenging the Text

9. The murder of Macduff's small son is one of the most pitiful and shocking scenes in Shakespeare. Do you think it might have been better to have it reported after the fact rather than to have shown the carnage onstage? What would be lost and what would be gained by this change?

*Drama Study Guide: **The Tragedy of Macbeth***

## Literary Elements Worksheet, Act IV

## Characterization

Most playwrights develop their characters through **indirect characterization.** That is, they do not tell us directly what a character is like but develop the character through his or her own words and actions. In addition, the audience has the opinions of other characters in the play to use in forming an impression of the character.

## Understanding Characterization

Answer the following questions about Macbeth as we see him in Act IV.

1. What do Macbeth's actions reveal about his character when he visits the witches and orders the murder of Macduff's family?

   _____

   _____

   _____

   _____

2. What do we learn about Macbeth from his own words?

   _____

   _____

   _____

   _____

3. What do the opinions of other characters add to our picture of Macbeth's character?

   **a.** Malcolm _____

   _____

   _____

   _____

   **b.** Macduff _____

   _____

   _____

   _____

ACT IV

*(Continued on page 76.)*

*Drama Study Guide: **The Tragedy of Macbeth***

*(Continued from page 75.)*

**4.** This is the only act in which there is no scene between Macbeth and Lady Macbeth. Why do you think this might be so?

_____

_____

_____

_____

## Applying Skills

Compare Macbeth's aside in Act IV, Scene 1 (lines 144–156), with his aside in Act I, Scene 3 (especially lines 139–142 and 143–144), and his soliloquy in Act I, Scene 7 (lines 1–28). Trace the decline of Macbeth's moral character as shown in these lines.

_____

_____

_____

_____

_____

_____

_____

_____

_____

_____

_____

_____

_____

_____

_____

_____

_____

*Drama Study Guide: **The Tragedy of Macbeth***

# Test, Act IV

## Thoughtful Reading *(40 points)*

On the line provided, write the letter of the *best* answer to each of the following items. *(8 points each)*

_____ **1.** In response to Macbeth's questions, the witches

    **a.** tell him everything and predict the course of his entire life

    **b.** call upon the apparitions, who answer most of his questions but warn him not to probe too deeply

    **c.** conjure up the ghost of the king, who answers the questions

    **d.** attempt to intimidate Macbeth and threaten him with a curse

_____ **2.** When Macbeth hears that no one born of a woman will harm him, he decides to

    **a.** leave Macduff alone

    **b.** kill all the wives of his peers

    **c.** kill Macduff anyway

    **d.** kill everyone in line for the throne but spare their families

_____ **3.** Lady Macduff misses her last chance for escape, which comes when

    **a.** an anonymous messenger warns her to flee

    **b.** her son suggests a plot for their escape

    **c.** Ross defends her husband's good character

    **d.** the murderers make too much noise at the door

_____ **4.** When Ross joins Malcolm and Macduff in Scene 3, he says to Macduff, "Let not your ears despise my tongue forever, / Which shall possess them with the heaviest sound / That ever yet they heard." He means,

    **a.** Do not listen too closely to what I am saying.

    **b.** I am about to warn you of impending disaster.

    **c.** Please do not hate me because I bring bad news.

    **d.** Do not worry about my next statement.

_____ **5.** When Macduff receives the news of his family, Malcolm urges him to

    **a.** rouse his anger           **c.** stay away from Scotland

    **b.** grieve peacefully         **d.** try not to think about it

## Expanded Response *(30 points)*

**6.** Which of the following characters in Act IV arouses the most sympathy? On the lines provided, write the letter of the character you choose, describe the character's situation in Act IV, and give reasons for your opinion. Use at least one example from the play to support your ideas. There is more than one possible answer. *(15 points)*

    **a.** Macbeth     **b.** Lady Macduff     **c.** son of Macduff     **d.** Macduff

_____

_____

_____

_____

*(Continued on page 78.)*

*Drama Study Guide: **The Tragedy of Macbeth***

ACT IV

*(Continued from page 77.)*

**7.** In the center column of the following chart, use your imagination combined with your knowledge of the events of the play thus far to describe events that you think each apparition might be predicting. In the right-hand column, explain the reason(s) for the events you described. *(15 points)*

| Apparition | What Might Happen | Why? |
|---|---|---|
| An Armed Head | | |
| A Bloody Child | | |
| A Crowned Child with a Tree in His Hand | | |

# Written Response *(30 points)*

**8.** On a separate sheet of paper, write a paragraph describing how Macbeth changes from the beginning of the play to Act IV. Is he more good than evil in Act IV? more evil than good? half good and half evil? Rate Macbeth's moral character on a scale of good to evil. Provide at least two examples of Macbeth's words or deeds to support your answer.

*Drama Study Guide: **The Tragedy of Macbeth***

# Graphic Organizer for Active Reading, Act V

## Truth and Consequences

The showdown between Macbeth and his enemies occurs in Act V. The prophecies the witches made in Act IV also come true. In the diagram below, describe each apparition that appears in Act IV. You may use words, symbols, or sketches to portray each apparition. Then, summarize each apparition's prediction, and explain how each prediction comes true.

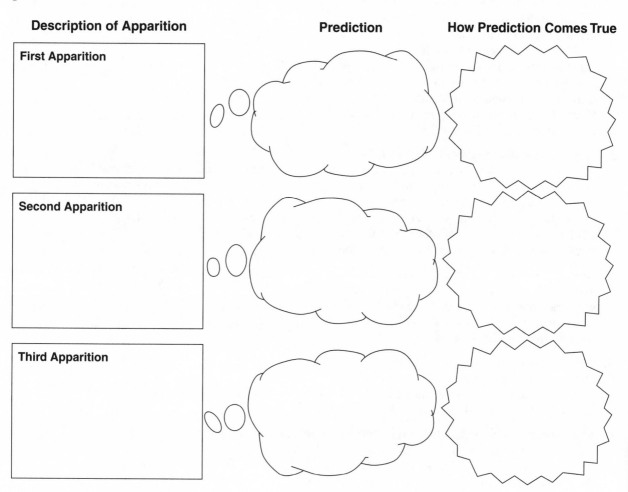

| Description of Apparition | Prediction | How Prediction Comes True |

**First Apparition**

**Second Apparition**

**Third Apparition**

1. Just before each prediction comes true, Macbeth realizes that it is accurate and that he cannot escape his fate. How does he cope with these realizations?

    _____

    _____

2. Does Macbeth make his fate more painful by demanding that the witches tell him his future? Explain why or why not.

    _____

    _____

ACT V

*Drama Study Guide: **The Tragedy of Macbeth***

# Making Meanings, Act V

## First Thoughts

1. How do you feel about what happens to Macbeth's body after he is dead?

## Shaping Interpretations

2. Theatrically, the spectacle of Lady Macbeth walking in her sleep is one of the most striking scenes in the play. It is entirely Shakespeare's invention, not found or suggested in his source. Why do you suppose Shakespeare has her walk in her sleep? How is this scene related to the remarks that Macbeth makes about sleep in Act II, Scene 2, just after he kills Duncan?

3. In the sleepwalking scene, Lady Macbeth refers to many of her waking experiences. For example, the words "One: two" may refer to the moment in Act II, Scene 1, when she struck the bell, signaling Macbeth to go and kill Duncan. Find traces of other experiences in what she says and does while sleepwalking.

4. At the end of Act IV, Malcolm says, "The night is long that never finds the day." In what metaphorical sense does he use the terms *night* and *day*? How does his remark **foreshadow** the outcome of the play?

5. The last act of *Macbeth* contains the play's **climax**—the most emotional and suspenseful part of the action—the moment when the characters' conflicts are finally resolved. Which part of Act V do you consider the climax? Explain.

6. Shakespeare gave most of his **tragic heroes** an impressive dying speech in which they say something significant about their own life and death. Although he did not write such a speech for Macbeth, which speech of Macbeth's do you think serves in the play as his dying speech? Why have you selected this speech rather than some other one?

---

### Reviewing the Text

a. Why, according to the doctor, is Lady Macbeth walking in her sleep?

b. In Scene 2, what opinion of Macbeth do the Scottish lords now hold?

c. When does Lady Macbeth die?

d. What is Macbeth's plan for dealing with the attacking troops? Why has he been forced to choose this plan?

e. What changes in his personality does Macbeth describe in Scene 5, lines 9–15?

f. In the speech in Scene 5 that begins "Tomorrow, and tomorrow, and tomorrow" (lines 19–28), how does Macbeth describe life? What metaphors does he use?

g. How are the prophecies proclaimed by the three apparitions in Act IV, Scene 1, fulfilled in Act V?

h. At the end of the play, what has become of Macbeth? Who becomes king?

---

## Connecting with the Text

7. What are your reactions to the idea expressed by Macbeth that life "is a tale / Told by an idiot, full of sound and fury, / Signifying nothing" (Scene 5, lines 26–28)? Explain your response.

## Challenging the Text

8. Sometime shortly after 1660, a playwright named William Davenant (who claimed to be a natural son of Shakespeare) added another sleepwalking scene to *Macbeth*: He had the ghost of Duncan chase Lady Macbeth about the stage. How might this scene change the way audiences perceive Lady Macbeth's character? Might it make the other ghosts in the play seem any more or less real? What might the scene add to the play, and what might it take away?

*Drama Study Guide: The Tragedy of Macbeth*

# Elements of Literature Mini-Lesson, Act V

## Imagery and Figurative Language

*Macbeth*'s poetry is rich in imagery and figurative language that help to create atmosphere and reveal character and theme.

1.  Powerful images in the play contrast the natural and the unnatural, as in this speech by Lady Macbeth:

    . . . I have given suck, and know
    How tender 'tis to love the babe that milks me:
    I would, while it was smiling in my face,
    Have plucked my nipple from his boneless gums,
    And dashed the brains out, had I so sworn as you
    Have done to this.
    —Act I, Scene 7, lines 54–59

    a.  What unnatural sounds and events are reported in Act II, Scenes 2–4? What mood do these images create?

    b.  Look at the witches' scenes. What would you say is the emotional effect of each scene? Besides the witches themselves, what unnatural images occur in these scenes?

2.  We hear about sleep and sleeplessness throughout the play. How is sleep described in these figures of speech?

    **a. First Witch.**
    I'll drain him dry as hay:
    Sleep shall neither night nor day
    Hang upon his penthouse lid. . . .
    —Act I, Scene 3, lines 18–20

    **b. Macbeth.**
    Methought I heard a voice cry "Sleep no more!
    Macbeth does murder sleep"—the innocent sleep,
    Sleep that knits up the raveled sleave of care,
    The death of each day's life, sore labor's bath,
    Balm of hurt minds, great nature's second course,
    Chief nourisher in life's feast—
    —Act II, Scene 2, lines 34–39

3.  Choose one of the following images, and find three speeches (from different scenes in the play) in which the image occurs:

    blood          darkness          disease          planting

    Look back at the context of each speech (what happens just before and after). What is the emotional effect of each one?

ACT V

*Drama Study Guide: The Tragedy of Macbeth*

# How to Own a Word Mini-Lesson, Act V

## Mapping: Increasing Your Vocabulary

If you draw on your own knowledge and experience when learning a new word, the word more readily becomes a part of your working vocabulary. **Mapping** is a vocabulary-building strategy that encourages active participation. Mapping works like this: First you see a new word used in a sentence. Before you look up the dictionary definition, you guess the word's meaning. After you look up the word in the dictionary, you use the word in a sentence of your own and become familiar with its different forms. An example of mapping appears on the right.

Here are some helpful suggestions for using mapping as one of your vocabulary-building strategies:

1. Scan your memory banks to remember whether you've heard the word before. Maybe you've heard a word that sounds similar to it.

2. Are there any clues in the sentence? In the example above, Macbeth seems surprised that something corporal could suddenly vanish into thin air. What does that suggest about the word's meaning?

3. Try substituting your guess for the word. Does it make sense in the context?

( corporal )

> **Banquo.**
>   . . . Whither are they vanished?
> **Macbeth.**
>   Into the air, and what seemed
>   **corporal** melted
>   As breath into the wind.

> **Your guess:** Something solid.
> Corpse, meaning "dead body," is a
> word that sounds similar. Perhaps
> there's some relation.

> **Definition:** of the body; bodily.

( Other forms: corporally (adv.) )

> **Your sentence: Corporal** punishment
> in schools has often been the subject of heated debates.

4. When you look up the word in the dictionary, make sure you read all the definitions. Select the one that fits best: Make sure that it's the right part of speech. *Corporal,* for example, can also refer to an officer in the army. But that definition doesn't work here: It's a noun. You're looking for an adjective in this context.

5. Think about the other forms of the word for a few moments. You might also want to use them in some sentences.

### Try It Out

In each sentence below, the vocabulary word is given in boldface. Using the mapping example for the word *corporal* as a guide, draw your own map for each of the following words.

1. **Macbeth.**
   . . . Thou sure and firm-set earth,
   Hear not my steps, which way they walk, for fear
   Thy very stones **prate** of my whereabout,
   And take the present horror from the time,
   Which now suits with it.
   —Act II, Scene 1, lines 56–60

2. **Lady Macbeth.**
   **Infirm** of purpose!
   Give me the daggers. The sleeping and the dead
   Are but as pictures. 'Tis the eye of childhood
   That fears a painted devil.
   —Act II, Scene 2, lines 51–54

3. **Macbeth.**
   Will all great Neptune's ocean wash this blood
   Clean from my hand? No; this my hand will rather
   The **multitudinous** seas incarnadine,
   Making the green one red.
   —Act II, Scene 2, lines 59–62

4. **Macduff.**
   Confusion now hath made his masterpiece.
   Most **sacrilegious** murder hath broke ope
   The Lord's anointed temple, and stole thence
   The life o' th' building.
   —Act II, Scene 3, lines 64–67

*Drama Study Guide: The Tragedy of Macbeth*

## Language Link Worksheet, Act V

### Active Voice and Passive Voice

A verb is in the **active voice** when it expresses an action performed by its subject. It is in the **passive voice** when it expresses an action done to its subject or when the subject results from the action.

> **ACTIVE VOICE:** The witches **made** a brew.
> **PASSIVE VOICE:** A brew **was made** by the witches.

A verb in the passive voice is usually less forceful than a verb in the active voice. Because of this a string of verbs in the passive voice can make your writing awkward and weak. Do not avoid the passive voice entirely, but use it sparingly. The active voice is usually the better choice. It is more direct than the passive voice. The active voice is also less wordy because a verb in the passive voice needs both a form of *to be* and a main verb. Often, as in the passive-voice sentence above, the preposition *by* is also needed.

Occasionally, a verb in the passive voice is best. Use the passive voice in the following cases:

| |
|---|
| You don't know who performed the action you are describing in your sentence. <br>     **EXAMPLE:** The tale of the witches **has been told** for years. |
| You don't want to reveal who performed the action. <br>     **EXAMPLE:** The king **was killed** while he was sleeping. |
| You want to spotlight the receiver of the action. <br>     **EXAMPLE:** Lady Macbeth **was pleased** by Macbeth's gruesome deeds. |
| You want to emphasize that the receiver of the action was a passive (often unwilling) recipient of the action. <br>     **EXAMPLE:** Macbeth **was** strongly **encouraged** to confess. |

Remember: As a general rule, use the active voice unless you have one of the above reasons to use the passive voice.

### EXERCISE A    Identifying Active and Passive Voice

In the blank before each sentence, write *A* if the italicized verb or verb phrase is in the active voice and *P* if the italicized verb or verb phrase is in the passive voice.

_____ **1.** Macbeth sees the apparitions and *interprets* them.

_____ **2.** He *is horrified* by the cries of the bloody child.

_____ **3.** The parade of kings *is passing* before Macbeth.

_____ **4.** The witches *warn* Macbeth to beware many things.

_____ **5.** Macbeth *is told* by Lennox that Macduff fled to England.

_____ **6.** Lady Macduff's son *is murdered* before her eyes.

_____ **7.** Lady Macbeth *washes* her hands constantly.

_____ **8.** Macduff *is saddened* by the recent events that have taken place in Scotland.

*(Continued on page 84.)*

*Drama Study Guide: The Tragedy of Macbeth*

    **83**

**ACT V**

*(Continued from page 83.)*

_____  **9.** Malcolm and the doctor *tell* Macduff that the king's blessing has the power to cure.

_____  **10.** Macduff *blames* himself when he hears of the deaths of his wife and children.

**EXERCISE B**    **Rewriting Sentences Using the Active Voice**

On the lines provided, rewrite the following sentences by changing the verbs in the passive voice to the active voice. Add new words if they are needed.

**1.** The witches' brew is thought by them to be a powerful mixture.

_____

**2.** Macbeth is told by the apparition not to worry until Birnam Wood comes to Dunsinane.

_____

**3.** The murderers are sent by Macbeth to kill the family of Macduff.

_____

**4.** Malcolm claims that he is ruled by sinful passions, lust, and avarice.

_____

**5.** Malcolm is comforted by Macduff's professions of loyalty.

_____

**EXERCISE C**    **Revising Paragraphs Using the Active Voice**

On a separate sheet of paper, revise the following paragraphs by changing verbs in the passive voice to the active voice. You may also have to change other words or move words. If you think that a sentence should remain in the passive voice, do not change it. Make any other changes that you think will improve the paragraphs.

Several great tragedies were written by Shakespeare. One of them, *Macbeth,* was written in 1606. This play was loosely based on historical events. In *Macbeth,* as in his other tragedies, the problems of character, morality, and free will were explored by Shakespeare.

The messages of *Macbeth* are still relevant today, and it is a powerful play. Many questions may be pondered by the reader: Why is power desired by Macbeth and Lady Macbeth? Why and how are people changed by events? How are crimes lived with by the criminals who commit them? The answers to such questions can assist the reader in understanding not only the play but also some current events.

*Drama Study Guide: **The Tragedy of Macbeth***

## Literary Elements Worksheet, Act V

### Elements of the Play

In Shakespeare's time great importance was placed on the natural order of things: the ranking of people in society, the order of the universe, and a human being's place in nature. Any disturbance in the natural order was thought to set off a chain reaction of chaos and unnatural events.

### Understanding Elements of the Play

Answer the following questions.

1. What unnatural occurrence sets the play in motion?

_____

_____

2. What central action in the play violates the natural order? In what specific ways does it do so?

_____

_____

_____

_____

3. What chaos does this action unleash? Name at least six "unnatural" consequences.

_____

_____

_____

_____

_____

_____

_____

4. How is the natural order restored at the end of the play?

_____

_____

_____

_____

_____

ACT V

(Continued on page 86.)

*Drama Study Guide:* **The Tragedy of Macbeth**

*(Continued from page 85.)*

## Applying Skills

How is the idea of order versus chaos or the natural versus the unnatural order consistent with the theme of the play?

_____

_____

_____

_____

_____

_____

_____

_____

_____

### Reader's Response

Which character in the play do you find most sympathetic? Why? Use at least two examples from the play to support your opinion.

_____

_____

_____

_____

_____

_____

_____

_____

_____

_____

*Drama Study Guide: **The Tragedy of Macbeth***

# Test, Act V

## Thoughtful Reading (40 points)

On the line provided, write the letter of the *best* answer to each of the following items. *(8 points each)*

_____ **1.** The gentlewoman in Scene 1 refuses to repeat Lady Macbeth's sleep talk to the doctor because

    **a.** the words are mumbled and impossible to understand
    **b.** Lady Macbeth forbade her to reveal the murders to anyone
    **c.** there is no witness to confirm the truth of the gentlewoman's words
    **d.** she thinks that only the doctor will believe her

_____ **2.** Macbeth tries to reassure himself that Malcolm and Macduff are not a threat to him because they

    **a.** are far away in England     **c.** have fled out of fear
    **b.** do not have the military power he has     **d.** are both "of woman born"

_____ **3.** As Macbeth's anxiety grows, he asks the doctor to

    **a.** let Lady Macbeth rest for a few days     **c.** medicate Lady Macbeth with hemlock
    **b.** cure Lady Macbeth and the country     **d.** analyze Lady Macbeth's ramblings

_____ **4.** Macbeth's reaction to his wife's death shows that he

    **a.** thinks life is a meaningless path to death
    **b.** is anguished because he cares about her deeply
    **c.** expects to win the battle without her support
    **d.** understands why she incited him to murder and then went mad

_____ **5.** Macduff declares that he must kill Macbeth because

    **a.** the witches predicted that he would     **c.** he must avenge the murder of his family
    **b.** no one else can conquer Macbeth     **d.** otherwise Macbeth will win the battle

## Expanded Response (30 points)

**6.** Which of the following quotations *best* represents the mood at the end of the play? On the lines provided, write the letter of the quotation you choose and explain your selection. Each quotation is a valid choice. Use at least one example from the play to support your ideas. *(15 points)*

    **a.** Siward: "Some must go off; and yet, by these I see, / So great a day as this is cheaply bought."

    **b.** Macduff: "The time is free."

    **c.** Malcolm: "I would the friends we miss were safe arrived."

    **d.** Malcolm: "So thanks to all at once and to each one, / Whom we invite to see us crowned. . . ."

_____

_____

_____

_____

_____

ACT V

*(Continued on page 88.)*

*Drama Study Guide: The Tragedy of Macbeth*

*(Continued from page 87.)*

7. Match each of the following quotations to its speaker. Below each speaker's name, write the letter of the appropriate quotation(s), and describe the speaker's emotional state when the words were spoken. Note: One speaker has two quotations. *(15 points)*

| Quotation | Speaker's Emotional State |
|---|---|
| **a.** "All the perfumes of Arabia will not sweeten this little hand." | Macbeth |
| **b.** "My voice is in my sword, thou bloodier villain / Than terms can give thee out!" | |
| | Lady Macbeth |
| **c.** "Accursèd be that tongue that tells me so, / For it hath cowed my better part of man!" | |
| | Macduff |
| **d.** "Out, damned spot! Out, I say!" | |

## Written Response *(30 points)*

8. Are the deaths in Act V of Lady Macbeth, Young Siward, and Macbeth inevitable? Choose one of these three characters. On a separate sheet of paper, write a paragraph describing the circumstances of his or her death, and explain whether you think the death was or was not inevitable and why.

*Drama Study Guide: **The Tragedy of Macbeth***

# Making Meanings, the Play as a Whole

## Shaping Interpretations

1. "Nothing in his life / Became him like the leaving it," says Malcolm in Act I, referring to the traitorous Thane of Cawdor. Malcolm also says that this Thane of Cawdor threw away the dearest thing he owned. How might these two statements also apply to Macbeth? Have you known, or do you know of, other people to whom these lines apply?

2. One of the **themes** of *Macbeth* centers on evil, which Shakespeare saw as a force beyond human understanding. Do you think Shakespeare also saw evil as stronger than the forces of good? Support your answer with events from the play.

3. How does Shakespeare keep his audience from losing all sympathy for and interest in Macbeth in spite of Macbeth's increasing viciousness? Were you in sympathy with Macbeth throughout the play, or was there a point at which you lost sympathy? If so, where?

4. One critic has observed that part of Macbeth's tragedy is the fact that many of his strengths are also his weaknesses. Explain this apparent contradiction. What are Macbeth's strengths? Which ones also work against him?

5. Think of a single event, at any time during the course of the play, that could have averted Macbeth's tragic end. What might this event have been? How could it have come about? How would it affect the outcome of the play?

6. **Internal conflicts** rage within Macbeth; he also experiences **external conflicts** with other characters. Explain some of the play's main conflicts, and trace their resolution.

## Extending the Text

7. What modern figure, real or fictional, had a downfall, like Macbeth's, that came after an attempt to gain great power? How is this modern figure like Macbeth, and how different? Would this modern figure make a good **tragic hero**?

## Challenging the Text

8. Do you think people should parody a great tragic play like *Macbeth,* the way Richard Armour does in "Macbeth and the Witches" (see the HRW Classics edition of *Macbeth,* pages 137–139)? Why or why not?

# Choices: Building Your Portfolio, the Play as a Whole

## Critical Writing

### 1. Monster or Not?

Lady Macbeth is sometimes regarded as a monster, ruthlessly ambitious and fiendishly cruel. What clues can you find in the play to suggest that Shakespeare did not want us to judge her so severely? In an essay, analyze her character as it is revealed through her words and actions and her relationship with Macbeth.

## Critical Writing

### 2. Probing Shakespeare's Mind

When Macbeth discovers how Macduff entered the world (Act V, Scene 8), he also discovers that the witches are "juggling fiends" who have given him a false sense of security. Why do you think Shakespeare shows Macbeth taken in by their prophecies? What might Shakespeare be implying about Macbeth's character? about the witches' powers? Write your answer in one or two paragraphs.

## Oral Interpretation

### 3. Say the Soliloquy

With a small group, select one of Macbeth's soliloquies and "perform" it in the way a choir interprets a song: Vary voice pitches, volume, tempo, rhythm, meter, and tone. Repeat key lines as a refrain, and use echoing words, vocal sound effects, harmony, and chanting to accentuate and enhance the words.

## Critical Thinking/Speaking

### 4. For the Defense

Imagine that Macbeth, instead of being killed, is brought to trial by a jury of his peers. Plan both a prosecution and a defense, with various class members taking the parts of Macbeth, at least four witnesses (two for each side), and lawyers for each side. Examine and cross-examine all witnesses, who must remain true to the facts of the play in their responses. Have both sides present closing arguments, and use classmates as jurors.

## Creative Writing

### 5. Witty Writing

A **parody** imitates a work of literature, art, or music in order to amuse or instruct. Parodies make a serious work seem ridiculous by exaggerating its style and language or by applying the style and language to inappropriate subject matter. Richard Armour's parody of the three weird sisters, "Macbeth and the Witches" (the HRW Classics edition of *Macbeth,* pages 137–139), gently pokes fun at Shakespeare. Choose another scene from the play, and write your own parody of it. Remember that you can use clever puns and nonsense words, as well as exaggeration, to make your parody humorous.

## Critical Thinking

### 6. An Emotional Examination

Thomas de Quincey writes that for him the comical scene with the porter produced the opposite effect, "a peculiar awfulness and a depth of solemnity." In his essay "On the Knocking at the Gate in *Macbeth*" (the HRW Classics edition of *Macbeth,* pages 132–134), he explores the cause of the tension he experienced in this scene. Find a scene in *Macbeth* that had a strong emotional effect on you. Carefully examine it to find out what caused this effect. Make a two-column chart on which you list words and actions from the play in one column and your responses in the other.

## Critical Thinking

### 7. Placing Macbeth in the Hot Seat

Look back at the excerpt from *The Inferno of Dante* in the HRW Classics edition of *Macbeth* (pages 140–147). Although Brutus and Cassius have leading roles in Shakespeare's *Julius Caesar,* Dante clearly did not regard them as heroes. What do you think Dante's attitude would have been toward Macbeth? Do you think he would have reserved a place in his version of hell especially for Macbeth? Write a paragraph explaining your response. Make sure to support it by citing specific details from the play.

*Drama Study Guide: The Tragedy of Macbeth*

## Test, the Play as a Whole

## Responding to Literature *(100 points)*

**1.** Several characters in *The Tragedy of Macbeth* must make difficult choices. Choose one character in the play. In the chart below, describe the character's options, and then describe what the character decides to do. *(25 points)*

| Character: | |
|---|---|
| **Character's Options** | **Character's Decision** |
| | |

**2.** *The Tragedy of Macbeth* is laden with imagery and figurative language. In the right-hand column of the chart, identify ways the following examples contribute to the play's mood and theme. *(25 points)*

| Examples | Contributions |
|---|---|
| Imagery:<br><br>nature in revolt (violent winds, foaming waves, and so on) | |
| Figurative language:<br><br>"There the grown serpent lies; the worm that's fled / Hath nature that in time will venom breed, / No teeth for th' present." | |

*(Continued on page 92.)*

*Drama Study Guide: The Tragedy of Macbeth*

*(Continued from page 91.)*

Respond to each of the questions below. Use an extra sheet of paper if necessary. *(25 points each)*

**3.** Give your interpretation of Lennox's comment that his country suffers "under a hand accursed" Then, explain how your interpretation of Lennox's remark relates to the events, characters, and themes of *Macbeth.*

_____

_____

_____

_____

_____

_____

_____

_____

_____

**4.** Does Macbeth fit the definition of a tragic hero? Write a paragraph in which you state and explain your answer. Make at least two references to the play to support your response.

_____

_____

_____

_____

_____

_____

_____

_____

_____

_____

*Drama Study Guide:* ***The Tragedy of Macbeth***

# Testing the Genre

## Reading a Shakespearean Drama

Carefully read the following excerpt from Act III, Scene 3, of *The Tragedy of Hamlet, Prince of Denmark*. Then, answer the questions that follow.

*Before the play opens, the king of Denmark had been murdered by his own brother, Claudius, who then assumed the crown and married the queen. Sometime later Prince Hamlet was visited by his father's ghost, who asked Hamlet to avenge the murder. Now Hamlet is waiting for an opportunity to kill his uncle, the new king. In this scene, Hamlet comes upon King Claudius as he is alone at his prayers.*

### FROM *The Tragedy of Hamlet* by William Shakespeare

| | | |
|---|---|---|
| **King.** | O, my offense is <u>rank</u>, it smells to heaven; | |
| | It hath the primal eldest curse upon't, | |
| | A brother's murder! Pray can I not, | |
| | Though inclination be as sharp as will. | |
| | My stronger guilt defeats my strong intent, | 5 |
| | And, like a man to double business bound, | |
| | I stand in pause where I shall first begin, | |
| | And both neglect. What if this cursed hand | |
| | Were thicker than itself with brother's blood, | |
| | Is there not rain enough in the sweet heavens | 10 |
| | To wash it white as snow? Whereto serves mercy | |
| | But to confront the visage of offense? | |
| | And what's in prayer but this twofold force, | |
| | To be <u>forestalled</u> ere we come to fall, | |
| | Or pardoned being down? Then I'll look up; | 15 |
| | My fault is past. But, O, what form of prayer | |
| | Can serve my turn? "Forgive me my foul murder"? | |
| | That cannot be; since I am still possessed | |
| | Of those effects for which I did the murder— | |
| | My crown, mine own ambition, and my queen. | 20 |
| | May one be pardoned and retain the offense? | |
| | In the <u>corrupted</u> currents of this world | |
| | Offense's gilded hand may shove by justice, | |
| | And oft 'tis seen the wicked prize itself | |
| | Buys out the law; but 'tis not so above. | 25 |
| | There is no shuffling; there the action lies | |
| | In his true nature,[1] and we ourselves compelled, | |
| | Even to the teeth and forehead of our faults, | |
| | To give in evidence. What then? What rests? | |
| | Try what repentance can. What can it not? | 30 |
| | Yet what can it when one can not repent? | |
| | O wretched state! O bosom black as death! | |
| | O limed[2] soul, that, struggling to be free, | |
| | Art more engaged! Help, angels! Make assay.[3] | |
| | Bow, stubborn knees; and heart with strings of steel, | 35 |
| | Be soft as <u>sinews</u> of the new-born babe! | |
| | All may be <u>well</u>.    [*Retires and kneels.*] | |

---

1. **there . . . nature:** in heaven the case is tried on its own merits.
2. **limed:** captured, as in birdlime.
3. **assay:** attempt; trial.

*(Continued on page 94.)*

*Drama Study Guide: **The Tragedy of Macbeth***

*(Continued from page 93.)*

[*Enter Hamlet.*]

**Hamlet.**  Now might I do it pat, now he is praying;
And now I'll do't. And so he goes to heaven,
And so am I revenged. That would be scanned.    40
A villain kills my father; and for that,
I, his sole son, do this same villain send
To heaven.
Why, this is hire and salary, not revenge!
He took my father grossly, full of bread,    45
With all his crimes broad blown, as flush as May;
And how his audit stands, who knows save heaven?
But in our circumstance and course of thought,
'Tis heavy with him; and am I then revenged,
To take him in the <u>purging</u> of his soul,    50
When he is fit and seasoned[4] for his passage?
No.
Up, sword, and know thou a more horrid hent.[5]
When he is drunk asleep; or in his rage;
Or in the incestuous pleasure of his bed;    55
At gaming, swearing, or about some act
That has no relish of salvation in't—
Then trip him, that his heels may kick at heaven,
And that his soul may be as damned and black
As hell, whereto it goes. My mother stays.    60
This physic but prolongs thy sickly days.    *Exit.*

**King.**  [*Rises.*] My words fly up, my thoughts remain below;
Words without thoughts never to heaven go.    *Exit.*

---

4. **seasoned:** here, ready; ripe.
5. **hent:** opportunity; occasion.

# Understanding Vocabulary *(20 points)*

Each underlined word below has also been underlined in the excerpt from *Hamlet*. Re-read those passages, and use context clues to help you select an answer. Write the letter of the word(s) that *best* complete(s) each sentence. *(4 points each)*

_____  **1.** A <u>rank</u> deed is one that is

  **a.** very important        **c.** foul
  **b.** heroic               **d.** ridiculous

_____  **2.** An action that is <u>forestalled</u> is

  **a.** prevented           **c.** approved
  **b.** encouraged          **d.** hastened

_____  **3.** A person who is <u>corrupted</u> is

  **a.** young and optimistic    **c.** vain and ambitious
  **b.** no longer innocent      **d.** likely to boast

_____  **4.** If you develop your <u>sinews</u>, you will be

  **a.** fit and strong         **c.** wealthy and powerful
  **b.** wise beyond your years  **d.** sympathetic to others

*(Continued on page 95.)*

*Drama Study Guide: **The Tragedy of Macbeth***

*(Continued from page 94.)*

_____ **5.** If you are <u>purging</u> something, you are

    **a.** enlarging it                **c.** criticizing it

    **b.** punishing it                **d.** cleansing it

## Thoughtful Reading *(35 points)*

On the line provided, write the letter of the *best* answer to each of the following items. *(7 points each)*

_____ **6.** When the king says, "My stronger guilt defeats my strong intent," he means that

    **a.** he intends to relieve his guilt through fervent prayer

    **b.** his guilt makes it difficult for him to be a strong king

    **c.** his sense of guilt is stronger than his desire to pray

    **d.** his sense of guilt is stronger than his ambition

_____ **7.** The lines "Is there not rain enough in the sweet heavens / To wash it white as snow?" contain an example of

    **a.** an external conflict            **c.** irony

    **b.** a simile                     **d.** a metaphor

_____ **8.** Hamlet decides not to kill the king as he prays because

    **a.** Hamlet would rather kill the king while he is sinning so that his soul will be damned

    **b.** Hamlet is afraid that he will be damned for killing a man while he is praying

    **c.** Hamlet wants to accuse and kill the king in public

    **d.** Hamlet wants to challenge the king to a duel

_____ **9.** In their speeches the king and Hamlet use imagery of

    **a.** poison and disease          **c.** heaven and hell

    **b.** crime and punishment       **d.** food and drink

_____ **10.** The last two lines spoken by the king are an example of

    **a.** foreshadowing              **c.** dramatic irony

    **b.** internal rhyme             **d.** a rhyming couplet

## Expanded Response *(15 points)*

**11.** Which word below do you think *best* characterizes Hamlet in this excerpt? On the lines provided or on a separate sheet of paper, write the letter of the answer you choose, and briefly defend your choice. There is more than one possible answer. Use at least one example from the excerpt to support your ideas.

    **a.** vengeful     **b.** cunning     **c.** hesitant     **d.** decisive

_____

_____

_____

_____

_____

*(Continued on page 96.)*

*Drama Study Guide: **The Tragedy of Macbeth***

*(Continued from page 95.)*

## Written Response *(30 points)*

12. Hamlet, like Macbeth, is a tragic hero who kills a king and is himself killed. On a separate sheet of paper, write a paragraph comparing and contrasting Hamlet's and Macbeth's motives for regicide (murdering a king). Make at least two references to specific details in *The Tragedy of Macbeth* and the excerpt from *The Tragedy of Hamlet* to support your ideas.

_____

_____

_____

_____

_____

_____

_____

_____

_____

_____

_____

_____

_____

_____

_____

_____

_____

_____

_____

_____

*Drama Study Guide: **The Tragedy of Macbeth***

# English Language Worksheet

## Shakespeare's Language

On the line provided, write the letter of the *best* answer to each of the following items. *(10 points each)*

_____  1. We need annotations for reading Shakespeare's works because

    **a.** Shakespeare wrote in Middle English
    **b.** Shakespeare's works need to be translated into Modern English
    **c.** the meanings of some English words have changed since Shakespeare's day
    **d.** Shakespeare's language is so ornate that it requires explanation

_____  2. Shakespeare's use of contractions differs from today's because he

    **a.** did not contract verbs
    **b.** contracted some pronouns as well as other words
    **c.** contracted only pronouns
    **d.** contracted certain nouns as well as verbs

_____  3. We know that some pronunciations in Shakespeare's day differed from modern pronunciations. This is evident from our examination of

    **a.** contemporary grammar texts
    **b.** contemporary actor's manuals
    **c.** diaries of the time
    **d.** the iambic rhythm of the Shakespearean line

_____  4. The grammar of Shakespeare's time was

    **a.** exactly the same as ours
    **b.** essentially the same as ours, with numerous minor differences
    **c.** significantly different from ours
    **d.** completely different from ours

_____  5. In Shakespeare's time, *th-* pronoun forms (for example, *thou, thy, thine*) were used in speaking with

    **a.** close friends and social superiors (parents, bosses, kings)
    **b.** spouses only
    **c.** spouses, close friends, and social inferiors (servants, subjects)
    **d.** business acquaintances only

_____  6. In Shakespeare's time, verbs with the special ending *-st* were used when the subject was

    **a.** *he*
    **b.** *she*
    **c.** *thou*
    **d.** *it*

_____  7. Compared with the English spoken today, English in Shakespeare's era offered a wider choice of

    **a.** present participles
    **b.** past participles
    **c.** adjectives
    **d.** adverbs

*(Continued on page 98.)*

*Drama Study Guide: **The Tragedy of Macbeth***

*(Continued from page 97.)*

_____ **8.** One way in which Shakespeare's vocabulary was more complex than today's was in the number of words available to indicate

    **a.** time
    **b.** location
    **c.** motion
    **d.** age

_____ **9.** *Inkhorn* terms are words borrowed from

    **a.** the printing industry
    **b.** early Old English
    **c.** classical languages
    **d.** the fads of Shakespeare's day

_____ **10.** The trickiest words in Shakespeare's works are those that

    **a.** are derived from Latin
    **b.** are derived from Middle English
    **c.** are used for their impressive sounds
    **d.** look familiar but have different meanings today

# Cross-Curricular Activity

## Social Studies

### Assignment

Imagine that you are friends with a modern-day Macbeth. A citizen of Scotland, he has written a letter to you in which he details his plans to seize political power and wealth in the United States. (The modern-day Macbeth does not state in his letter that he plans to murder anyone to achieve his goals.)

This modern-day Macbeth owns a business in Scotland that exports whatnots to the United States. Macbeth is the only exporter of whatnots to the United States, but heavy export taxes are forcing him to raise his prices. His sales are therefore falling.

To eliminate this problem, the modern-day Macbeth plans to become president of the United States and eliminate the export tax on his whatnots. He even intends to enact a law that would prevent anyone else in the United States from making or selling whatnots.

The modern-day Macbeth assumes that he would not need to serve a four-year term as president. He plans to resign early and return to Scotland as soon as he becomes rich.

For this assignment, write a letter responding to the modern-day Macbeth's letter. Explain the checks and balances in our government that would make it extremely difficult for him to execute his plans.

### Gathering Information and Creating Your Letter

To review the system of checks and balances in the United States government that would impede the modern-day Macbeth's plans, consult an American government textbook. You may also look in a library catalog under such headings as

*United States politics; government; legislative branch; executive branch;* and *checks and balances.*

Make a written outline of points you want to include in your letter. Record the sources of any quotations, statistics, or opinions you plan to use. You do not need to cite the source of information that is general knowledge.

You might organize your information into two categories: problems the modern-day Macbeth would have becoming president and problems he would have creating and enacting laws. Then, organize your arguments in a logical order, ending with your most persuasive reason for the modern-day Macbeth to abandon his plans. Write a first draft of your letter.

### Sharing What You Learned

Exchange first drafts with another student. Help each other identify any problems in clarity, organization, or tone. Then, exchange constructive feedback on the persuasiveness of each other's arguments. Finally, revise your letter according to your partner's suggestions.

### Peer / Self-Evaluation

To evaluate your letter, consider whether you have clearly explained how the three branches of the federal government balance one another's power. Did you describe the powers over the executive branch that are granted by the Constitution to the legislative and judicial branches? Finally, do you think you persuaded the modern-day Macbeth to abandon his plans? Did you persuade him without insulting him? Why or why not?

*Drama Study Guide: The Tragedy of Macbeth*

# Read On

**The Day They Shot Lincoln** by Jim Bishop

Jim Bishop's careful retelling of a shocking assassination, *The Day They Shot Lincoln* chronicles a single day in the history of the United States, a day that changed the course of the nation. More than the story of a murder, Bishop's book is a powerful portrait of a nation—its leaders and its citizens, its past and its future.

**The Strange Case of Dr. Jekyll and Mr. Hyde** by Robert Louis Stevenson

Dr. Jekyll is a man respected for his honor and his generosity. Mr. Hyde is a brutal murderer. Can these two men be the same person? Robert Louis Stevenson's most disturbing tale, *The Strange Case of Dr. Jekyll and Mr. Hyde* explores the idea that good and evil can coexist in the same individual. Will one triumph and assume control over the other?

**Lord of the Flies** by William Golding

Are children innocent, or are they capable of evil? William Golding explores this question in *Lord of the Flies,* a best-selling novel. The story suggests that children, left to their own devices, will play out the roles—the good ones and the evil ones— they have learned in adult society. Stranded on a desert island after their plane crashes, Golding's schoolboys form their own society. Find out what happens as chaos and savagery seep into this new world. You may also want to see Peter Brook's 1963 film adaptation of the novel.

**The Crucible** by Arthur Miller

*The Crucible,* Arthur Miller's 1953 play about the Salem witchcraft trials of 1692, is considered by some to be a bitter indictment of another "witch hunt"—Senator Joseph McCarthy's hunt for Communist sympathizers. Miller's play dramatizes the effects of the fear and suspicion that fueled "the Red scare." When personal conscience is sacrificed to public ambition, when leaders become tyrants, the integrity of the nation suffers. In 1996, the play was adapted for the big screen; the movie stars Winona Ryder and Daniel Day-Lewis.

**The Lord of the Rings** by J.R.R. Tolkien

J.R.R. Tolkien's *The Lord of the Rings,* a trilogy, is the sequel to *The Hobbit.* In this work, Frodo the Hobbit is the reluctant heir to a magic ring— one that gives its wearer long life and tremendous power. But it also corrupts its wearer, and the story that unfolds chronicles the battles over little Frodo's magic ring, battles whose outcome will af-fect civilizations far and wide. In the battle between good and evil, who will triumph?

**Murder in the Cathedral** by T. S. Eliot

Like Shakespeare's plays, T. S. Eliot's play *Murder in the Cathedral* is written in verse. Set in medieval England, Eliot's drama tells the story of the assassination of Thomas à Becket, an archbishop of Canterbury. Becket opposed King Henry II's proposed limitations on the clergy, and for this he was murdered by four knights of Henry's court. In Eliot's version the king offers his friend and arch-bishop worldly power if he will give up his ideals, but to no avail. When good stands its ground, how-ever, evil resorts to drastic—and tragic—measures.

**Henry IV, Part I** by William Shakespeare

Shakespeare's history plays show just how turbulent politics have always been. *Henry IV, Part I,* depicts—you guessed it—the early years of the reign of Henry IV, years of political conflict. Henry Percy, otherwise known as Hotspur, threatens King Henry's dominion. The king's son, Prince Hal, is too busy making merry with the comic Falstaff and his band of revelers to come to his father's aid. In the end, though, Hal is called on to protect his fa-ther's sovereignty. Everything depends on the battle between Hal and Hotspur. Who will be vic-torious, and whose defeat will end in death?

**The Tragedy of Julius Caesar**
by William Shakespeare

Just pick up a newspaper or turn on the TV, and you'll see that the major themes of Shakespeare's *The Tragedy of Julius Caesar*—wars, terrorism, the use of propaganda to influence the masses, mob violence, assassinations—are relevant today. People are still swayed and even controlled by powerful and persuasive individuals and groups. How do we decide to join one group and oppose another? What do we do when appeals to our am-bition conflict with our sense of honor?

**Throne of Blood** directed by Akira Kurosawa

A tyrant's rise to power is an international theme. In 1957, the Japanese filmmaker Akira Kurosawa used Shakespeare's Scottish play to tell a story set in feudal Japan. In Kurosawa's *Throne of Blood,* a samurai, coaxed by his wife and an old witch, murders his lord at Cobweb Castle. With stunning visuals and a healthy dose of horror, Kurosawa demonstrates just how relevant Shakespeare can be—for people living at any time and in any place.

*Drama Study Guide: **The Tragedy of Macbeth***

# Answer Key

## Graphic Organizer for Active Reading, Act I

Responses will vary. Sample responses follow.

### Graphic Organizer

*The Good Macbeth:* He vigorously defends the king initially. When the witch's prediction that he will become Thane of Cawdor comes true, he has misgivings about the future. When he *does* form a plot to kill the king, he expresses reservations.

*Neutral/Ambiguous:* Macbeth passively receives the witches' news. He likes the idea of becoming king, but he has taken no action yet.

*The Evil Macbeth:* He talks with false affection to King Duncan. He views Malcolm, the king's son, not as a superior but only as a stumbling block. He conspires with Lady Macbeth to kill the king. At the end of Act I, he has no misgivings.

1. Many students will likely say that Macbeth would not have changed. The prospect of becoming king is so far from his mind that he might happily have served as Thane of Cawdor if the witches had not planted the idea in his mind. A few students may say that Macbeth's inherent greed would have taken him in an evil direction in any case.

2. Some students may say that all people are tempted by the prospect of power or wealth and would go to great lengths if they believed these things were readily attainable. Others may say that most people would not go so far as to plot murder to satisfy their greed and lust for power.

## Making Meanings, Act I

### Reviewing the Text

a. They plan to meet "upon the heath" in order "to meet with Macbeth" (Scene 1, lines 6–7).

b. Macbeth has beaten and beheaded Macdonwald and joined with Banquo to confront Sweno and the Norwegian forces to bring them to terms.

c. The king chooses to give Cawdor's title to Macbeth to reward him for saving the nation.

d. They name Macbeth Thane of Glamis and Cawdor and "king hereafter." They tell Banquo that he will be "lesser than Macbeth, and greater" and "Not so happy, yet much happier"

and that he'll "get kings, though thou be none" (lines 48–50, 65–67).

e. Responses will vary. Sample responses: Scene 5, lines 39–42, 51, 59–60; Scene 7, lines 61–72.

### First Thoughts

1. Responses will vary. Sample responses: She seems cruel, conniving, ambitious, bossy, devilish, evil, and clever. Their intimate greetings indicate that she and Macbeth are close; judging by the way she manipulates him, she is the stronger character in this relationship.

### Shaping Interpretations

2. This play may be about darkness and evil or about riddles or paradoxes. The weather reflects the stormy passions that will lead to a murderous plot.

3. Responses will vary. Sample response: That the first two prophecies turn out to be true leads Macbeth to contemplate murder to make the third true also (Scene 3, lines 127–142).

4. The phrase indicates that Banquo will be both less and greater than Macbeth, a seeming contradiction. Students will not know the truth of this until later in the play, but they may guess that it means Banquo will ultimately make greater contributions or receive more honor than Macbeth.

5. While Macbeth "start[s], and seem[s] to fear" (Scene 3, line 51), Banquo maintains his poise, neither begging nor fearing. Banquo wonders at their vanishing and is skeptical, but Macbeth longs for them to stay and commands them to speak. Macbeth seems superstitious and gullible.

6. He weighs his aversion to murdering Duncan against his desire to be king; he wonders whether to see what happens or make the third prophecy come true. When Duncan makes Malcolm his heir, Duncan directly blocks Macbeth's path to the throne, which tips the balance in favor of violence.

7. Responses will vary. Sample responses: Lady Macbeth—practical, single-minded, logical, strong; Macbeth—open to persuasion, poetic, sensitive, insecure when not in battle, argumentative, easily impressed. Lady Macbeth wins; Macbeth is persuaded.

*Drama Study Guide: The Tragedy of Macbeth*

**ANSWER KEY**

HRW MATERIAL COPYRIGHTED UNDER NOTICE APPEARING EARLIER IN THIS WORK.

**101**

**8.** The audience would feel dramatic irony: Duncan praises the place where, if his hosts have their way, he will be murdered.

## Extending the Text

**9.** *Synthesis.* It could be explained if Macbeth in fact has already wanted or plotted to become king. Possible evidence: Scene 3, line 51—a guilty conscience might be why he starts; lines 134–137—he immediately thinks of murder (though the witches say nothing of it and he did not murder to get the first two titles), perhaps because he has already considered it.

# Language and Style Mini-Lesson, Act I

### Blank Verse

**1.** Model passages in class to help students see the concept. Students will probably discover that the meter in Macbeth's speeches tends to be less regular than in Lady Macbeth's, which makes his dialogue sound more erratic and hers more calm or logical.

**2.** No. (Point out that the witches speak in tetrameter.) The style of the witches' speech separates their speech from that of other, more earthly characters. It emphasizes the incantation-like character of their speech.

**3.** There is only one: Scene 5, lines 1–13. It is a quotation from a letter Macbeth wrote in prose, so it is appropriate to keep it in prose.

# Language Link Worksheet, Act I

### Revision Worksheet

Revisions will vary. A sample revision follows.

### The Thane of Cawdor: Who Earned the Title?

At the conclusion of Act I, Scene 2, of *Macbeth,* Duncan decrees the execution of the traitorous Thane of Cawdor. Then the king directs Ross to "greet Macbeth" with the title. Duncan's decision is ironic because it is Macduff, not Macbeth, who deserves the honor.

Throughout the play, Ross is identified with Macduff. When Ross reports the events of the war to Duncan in Act I, Scene 2, he says that he comes from Fife, Macduff's castle. Ross announces that the Thane of Cawdor and the Norwegian king, Sweno, have been captured at Fife. It is logical to

assume, therefore, that the warrior whom Ross refers to as Bellona's bridegroom is Macduff. Later, in Act I, Scene 3, the witches address Macbeth with the words "Hail . . . Thane of Cawdor!" Confused, Macbeth rejects the title and describes the Thane of Cawdor as "a prosperous gentleman." Macbeth's response proves he knows nothing of the Thane of Cawdor's treachery and defeat. Indeed, Macbeth deserves to be rewarded by his king. Macbeth did defeat the traitor Macdonwald, beheading him and slitting his body open. It is Macduff, however, whose heroic victories over the Thane of Cawdor and the king of Norway are responsible for ending the war. It is both ironic and unjust that having earned the title, Macduff does not receive it.

# Literary Elements Worksheet, Act I

### Understanding Conflict

| | | | |
|---|---|---|---|
| **1.** external | | **5.** external | |
| **2.** external | | **6.** external | |
| **3.** internal | | **7.** internal | |
| **4.** internal | | **8.** external | |

### Applying Skills

Responses will vary. Students should note that the idea that every moral decision creates consequences is addressed in the play. In Act I, Scene 7, we see that Macbeth clearly knows that murdering Duncan will be a violent crime.

### Reader's Response

Responses will vary.

# Test, Act I

### Thoughtful Reading

**1.** b     **2.** c     **3.** b     **4.** b     **5.** a

### Expanded Response

**6.** Responses will vary. Students should use at least one example from the play to support their ideas. The best answers are **a, b,** and **c.** Sample responses follow.

   **a.** This quotation best describes the mood of deception and foreboding because nothing in Act I is as it seems. The fact that Macbeth is granted the title Thane of Cawdor *seems* positive, but because this event confirms the

*Drama Study Guide: **The Tragedy of Macbeth***

witch's prediction, it is also ominous. It is paradoxical and troubling that the witches, who are "foul," are the bearers of good news about Macbeth's and Banquo's future.

b. This quotation best describes the sinister mood of approaching violence. Evil darkness seems to be consuming Macbeth and Lady Macbeth.

c. This quotation best describes the mood of deception and foreboding. The "false face" of flattery and solicitude that Macbeth and his wife wear to deceive the king is like the false face that the previous Thane of Cawdor wore. The "false heart" of both Macbeth and Lady Macbeth is full of evil plans.

d. This answer is insupportable.

7. Responses will vary. Sample responses follow.

*Character Traits*—capacity for greed, craving for power and wealth, weakness in upholding moral beliefs.

*External Events*—the idea of being king (planted by the third witch), the witches' prophecies, Lady Macbeth's enthusiasm and goading.

## Written Response

8. Responses will vary. In a model response, students should fulfill the following criteria:
   - demonstrate understanding of the prompt
   - describe Macbeth's thoughts as he confirms his intent to carry out the plan. For example:
     - Macbeth hesitates because he is a "kinsman" and subject of the king and should be protecting rather than hurting the king.
     - The king is gentle and well liked by the people, and Macbeth could be caught and punished.
     - Macbeth dismisses his fears because his ambition is too great, because Lady Macbeth scolds him for his cowardliness, and because he thinks he can frame the king's attendants.
     - Macbeth rationalizes his decision by convincing himself that killing the king is the brave thing to do because he is concerned about his heirs.
   - support ideas with at least two references to the play (the previous examples are sufficient)

# Graphic Organizer for Active Reading, Act II

Responses will vary. Sample responses follow.

## Graphic Organizer

"But wherefore could not I pronounce 'Amen'? / I had most need of blessing, and 'Amen' / Stuck in my throat" (Scene 2, lines 30–32); Macbeth fears God and feels so guilty that he cannot request a blessing.

"I am afraid to think what I have done; / Look on't again I dare not" (Scene 2, lines 50–51); Macbeth is so horrified by the murders that he cannot look at the dead men again or even think of the slayings.

"Will all great Neptune's ocean wash this blood / Clean from my hand?" (Scene 2, lines 59–60); Macbeth realizes that although he may physically wash the blood away, the intangible and invisible effects—memories of his deed, his guilt, and his horror—will never be cleansed, no matter how "great" the ocean in which they are washed.

"To know my deed, 'twere best not know myself" (Scene 2, line 72); Macbeth, absorbed by thoughts of the killings, admits that it is better not to pursue self-knowledge because the deed was so gruesome—he is tortured by remorse and revulsion.

1. Students may say that Macbeth's general state of mind is tormented remorse.

2. Some students may state that Macbeth should confess, and atone for, his crimes. Others may say that Macbeth should continue hiding his deeds because he has gone too far—it is pointless to turn back.

# Making Meanings, Act II

## Reviewing the Text

a. He promises Banquo honor if Banquo will stand by him. Banquo agrees to support Macbeth as long as he can maintain his integrity while doing so.

b. Macbeth sees a dagger in the air that becomes coated with blood. This foreshadows the murder of Duncan.

c. Lady Macbeth hears an owl scream and crickets cry. Macbeth hears Malcolm and Donalbain laugh and cry "Murder" in their sleep and say "God bless us!" and "Amen." He also hears a voice cry that "Macbeth doth murder sleep."

d. The sleeping Duncan resembles her father. She comes up with the plan, lays the daggers ready, returns the daggers, smears the grooms with

*Drama Study Guide: The Tragedy of Macbeth*

HRW MATERIAL COPYRIGHTED UNDER NOTICE APPEARING EARLIER IN THIS WORK.

103

blood, and plans the cleanup—washing hands and donning nightgowns.

e. He says it will never wash off—it will stain all the waters of the world.

f. He is pretending that he is the porter to hell.

g. He has come to wake the king, as he was requested to do.

h. He says he killed the guards out of love for Duncan.

i. Malcolm goes to England; Donalbain goes to Ireland.

j. Students may find this unclear. Point out that Macduff says, perhaps ironically, that Malcolm and Donalbain are guilty (lines 24–27), but then he skips Macbeth's coronation, possibly because he already suspects Macbeth.

## First Thoughts

1. Responses will vary. Sample responses: It is awful. I wish I knew how the third prophecy could have been fulfilled if Macbeth had decided not to kill Duncan. The murders may be committed offstage because they are too bloody and upsetting; seeing the murders would take the focus off Macbeth and demand more sympathy for Duncan.

## Shaping Interpretations

2. The character is Malcolm in Scene 3, lines 135–137, or Macduff in Scene 3, line 105 (he questions Macbeth's killing of the grooms), Scene 4, lines 24–27 (a remark that may be ironic) and 36 (he plans to skip Macbeth's coronation).

3. Perhaps she talks a better game than she plays; she is not as insensitive as she'd like to be.

4. It could be intended as a lie, but it is more likely an equivocation, an ambiguous sentiment. It may be true that Macbeth will never again feel that anything is worthwhile—he has ruined his own life in taking Duncan's. In this case the speech would be true, but not as the hearers understand it, as a lament for Duncan. Macbeth is nervous about discovery (Scene 3, line 51) and feels guilty (Scene 3, line 59), though not guilty enough to confess.

5. She wants to convey shock and grief.

6. He is courteous, dutiful, loyal, sensitive, poetic, thoughtful, discerning, bold, wary, impulsive.

7. The mood is sinister and violent. It is set by the dagger vision and what follows (Scene 1, lines 33–61), the image of Duncan dead (Scene 3,

lines 109–112), the cannibal horses (Scene 4, lines 14–18). Blood and water might symbolize death and life or guilt and innocence.

## Extending the Text

8. *Synthesis.* Responses will vary. Sample responses: Macduff is horrified; Malcolm and Donalbain are in shock—they do not really feel grief yet and still feel themselves in too much danger to release their feelings; Lennox seems overwhelmed. Some people today would be horrified; some would flee the country; because people have been desensitized by seeing so much violence in the modern media, some might not be so surprised.

## Challenging the Text

9. *Synthesis.* Responses will vary. Sample responses: The Old Man, who does not appear elsewhere, makes the scene seem less connected to the others; the scene summarizes what is already known. The scene reinforces the sense of building suspicions and indicates that Macduff does not attend the coronation. Perhaps the Old Man represents wisdom or is someone who has come to warn the others about associating with evildoers.

10. *Evaluation.* Responses will vary. Some students may believe the porter scene is designed to contrast sharply with the deed of the Macbeths; they will therefore agree with De Quincey that the author's intent is to set the Macbeths apart and reacquaint readers with the real world.

# Words to Own Worksheet, Act II

## Developing Vocabulary

1. I will augment my meager allowance by mowing lawns during the summer.

2. It is a common stereotype that women prate whereas men are strong and silent.

3. I always associate the cheerful knell of bells with Christmastime.

4. The mad narrator told the story in a crazed, erratic fashion.

5. Although my grandmother has just turned eighty, neither her mind nor her body is infirm.

6. The holes in his jeans were as multitudinous as the stars in the sky.

7. The boss treated most of his workers in a rough manner, but he was always kind to me.

*Drama Study Guide: The Tragedy of Macbeth*

8. The priest explained to the children that to drink tap water from the sacred chalice would be to commit a sacrilegious act.

9. Steeped in culture, we left the museum only after we had thoroughly studied every painting in the exhibition.

10. After the war it was decided to entomb the unknown soldiers, and a great monument was built for the purpose.

# Literary Elements Worksheet, Act II

## Understanding Suspense

1. Answers may vary. Students should acknowledge that the expectation arose that Duncan will already have been killed or that his murder will begin Act II.

2. Macbeth seems overcome with dread at the thought of what he is about to do, and it seems possible that he may change his mind.

3. They raise the possibility that the grooms may wake up while the murder is in progress.

4. The grooms may wake up before they have been made to appear to be the murderers.

5. The reader wonders whether someone will enter and find Macbeth and Lady Macbeth awake with bloody hands.

6. Macduff is knocking at the gate.

7. The scene with the porter delays the discovery of the murder.

8. The audience or reader wonders what will happen to Macbeth next.

## Applying Skills

Answers will vary. Students should note that Malcolm suspects that Macbeth is capable of murder, which foreshadows the possibility that he will act on his suspicions. Malcolm also does not fully believe that Macbeth was saddened and shocked by Duncan's murder. The reader is left to wonder what Malcolm's actions and Macbeth's fate will be.

# Test, Act II

## Thoughtful Reading

**1.** c    **2.** a    **3.** b    **4.** d    **5.** c

## Expanded Response

6. The name of the speaker of each quotation is given below. Responses to the question of what

the quotations reveal will vary. Students should use at least one example from the play to support their ideas. All choices are supportable. Sample responses follow.

**a.** Lady Macbeth; she is cold and calculating—she has no interest in contemplating the murders because she believes such thoughts would make her insane.

**b.** Macbeth; he is humorous, almost indifferent, in his warning to Duncan to get his spiritual house in order. However, he is also well aware of heaven and hell—this foreshadows his later torment.

**c.** Lady Macbeth; she is neither compassionate nor sympathetic. She cruelly alerts Macbeth that his tortured thoughts of the murders are dishonorable.

**d.** Macduff; he is a good man who is genuinely appalled by the king's death. He is so shocked that he cannot speak or think about what has happened.

7. Responses will vary. Sample responses follow.

*Lady Macbeth's Remarks*—She attempts to persuade Macbeth that the victims are insubstantial and easily dismissed (she compares the sleeping and dead to mere pictures); she reassures Macbeth that the blood from his crimes is superficial and easily washed away; she instructs him not to think too much or to have remorse, as such thoughts will drive him mad; she compliments Macbeth (she calls him worthy and noble) to strengthen his pride and confidence.

*How the Remarks Help Lady Macbeth and Macbeth*—Lady Macbeth is not just trying to comfort her husband; she is also trying to allay her own fears and torments. She is not entirely successful in comforting Macbeth, but she seems to soothe herself effectively.

## Written Response

8. Responses will vary. In a model response, students should fulfill the following criteria:
   • demonstrate understanding of the prompt
   • describe the malevolent and violent mood of Act II
   • provide reasons for the mood. For example:
     • The king and the guards have been murdered.
     • Macbeth is suffering inner torment.
     • Macbeth has been deceiving others.
   • discuss why the mood is likely to prevail. For example:

*Drama Study Guide: **The Tragedy of Macbeth***

- The murders set in motion events that cannot have happy endings.
- The foreshadowing, such as the many references to madness, is ominous.
- support ideas with at least two examples from Act II (the previous examples are sufficient)

# Graphic Organizer for Active Reading, Act III

Responses will vary. Sample responses follow.

## Graphic Organizer

*Macbeth's Fear*—Macbeth fears that Banquo's heirs will gain the throne that Macbeth committed murder in order to attain.

*Events*—Macbeth plots to kill Banquo and his son, Fleance. The hired murderers fail to kill Fleance. Macbeth is haunted by Banquo's ghost.

*Banquet Scene*—Macbeth is the only one at the banquet who sees the ghost; he acts strangely, drawing attention to himself.

1. Students may assert that if Macbeth had not known that Banquo's sons were destined to succeed to the throne, he would not have perceived Banquo as a threat and perhaps would then have reigned longer and probably would not have killed him.

2. Some students may think that Macbeth should not try to control fate since he cannot change it, and any attempt to manipulate or accelerate his fate would be disastrous. Other students may say that Macbeth is right in trying to assert his free will despite the witches' prophecies—that he should take some control, illusive as that control may be.

# Making Meanings, Act III

## Reviewing the Text

a. Banquo suspects that Macbeth murdered Duncan. Although his thoughts are interrupted by Macbeth's arrival, he seems to be waiting to find out whether the rest of the prophecy comes true.

b. He hires two murderers and convinces them that Banquo wronged them. He then sends a third murderer to make sure that they do their job because Macbeth sees Banquo as a threat. Lady Macbeth is not involved in these plans.

c. Fleance escapes.

d. Macbeth (but no one else) sees Banquo's ghost at Macbeth's chair and speaks to him, refusing to sit. Lady Macbeth tries to cover for Macbeth by saying he customarily has fits; she dismisses the guests.

e. He has gone to the court of Edward, king of England, to ask for an army to help overthrow Macbeth.

f. They believe him guilty of the murders of Duncan and Banquo.

## First Thoughts

1. Responses will vary. Sample responses: "Botches in the Work" or "The Bloody Business" (taken from quotations).

## Shaping Interpretations

2. Responses will vary. Sample response: Perhaps he wanted to show a change in Macbeth's character—to show him not only growing accustomed to crime but also becoming more devious and arranging matters so he can deny that he did it and be technically honest (an equivocation).

3. Responses will vary. Sample responses: Some changes are role reversals—she plans the first murder, and he goes along only because of her plan; but he plans Banquo's murder, arranges to have it done by others, and keeps her out of it. They seem very intimate as they plan and carry out Duncan's murder; now she is not even in his confidence, and he does not share with or depend on her the way he did before. The changes in their relationship are some of the effects of committing murder; perhaps they have lost trust in each other as they constantly distrust those around them.

4. Responses will vary. Sample response: Macbeth's words indicate the time in which the scene takes place, probably dusk—a time when there is a blurring of distinction between light and dark—but in a metaphorical sense he comments on the blurring between good and evil. Several other remarks can also be taken as both literal and metaphorical. For example, in Scene 4, lines 126–127 again refer to the blurring of time in the scene and in the motif of reversal. Lines 78–83 are directed at the ghost literally but could also be taken metaphorically to mean that past misdeeds continue to haunt and "unseat" one.

5. Responses will vary. Students may say that it is the first time that Macbeth's plans have definitely gone awry, and it leaves open the

*Drama Study Guide: The Tragedy of Macbeth*

possibility that Banquo's descendants will be kings.

6. Responses will vary. Sample response: The scene plays upon the frightening possibility of madness. What seems to be real may not be, as Macbeth can see something no one else at the table can see. Also, if an actor plays the ghost, then a supernatural being is presented as if it existed, another blurring of the distinction. This effect also may apply in the witches' scenes and to the descriptions of the natural world's response to Duncan's murder.

7. Responses will vary. Students may say that she is pointing out that they have committed a terrible crime—in effect, sold their souls—and yet fulfilling their ambitions has not made them happy. Macbeth thinks it is still possible to achieve peace if only he can kill Banquo and Fleance.

8. Responses will vary. Sample responses: Have an actor play the ghost; use technology to project a ghost; use a strong light over the chair to suggest the ghost's presence; have the ghost be a figment of Macbeth's imagination. Banquo's ghost in the flesh blurs the distinction between the real and the imaginary, and it shows the strong influence murder can have on the mind of the murderer. Showing no ghost onstage emphasizes that Macbeth is hallucinating.

### Extending the Text

9. *Synthesis.* Responses will vary. Sample response: The guilty will be found and pay with their lives. It is relevant in regard to a discussion of the death penalty, as society must decide whether the murderer should pay with his or her life.

### Challenging the Text

10. *Evaluation.* Responses will vary. Sample responses: It may be one of the witches making sure Fleance escapes so the prophecy can come true. Or it may be Ross, Seyton, or Macbeth. It is not a flaw—it adds to the creepiness. It is a flaw because it distracts the audience's attention from more important issues.

## Literary Elements Worksheet, Act III

### Understanding Imagery

1. Macbeth compares the murderers to various canines that, regardless of their qualitative differences, are all classified as dogs.

2. Macbeth is uneasy about what he has done, and his conscience is bothering him.

3. When the "light thickens," the good things of day are gone, and evil takes over.

4. Macbeth refers to Banquo as a serpent and to Fleance as a worm.

5. He refers to his state of mind as a summer cloud that suddenly moves in front of the sun.

### Applying Skills

Responses will vary. Students should note that images about nature, light, and dark appear throughout Act III. Each contributes to the play's gloomy mood and the theme of evil coming back to haunt the evildoer.

## Test, Act III
### Thoughtful Reading

**1.** b  **2.** c  **3.** b  **4.** a  **5.** b

### Expanded Response

6. Responses will vary. Sample responses follow.

   *Act I*—Macbeth has misgivings. Lady Macbeth has no regrets and goads him to commit the crime.

   *Act II*—Macbeth is instantly remorseful. Lady Macbeth is determined to stick to their evil agenda.

   *Act III*—Macbeth is willing to murder again and feels guiltless. Lady Macbeth has misgivings.

   Both characters have changed because they have experienced the psychological consequences of crime. Macbeth feels he has sunk so low that he is beyond redemption or remorse. Lady Macbeth, who has not directly murdered anyone, feels that there is still time to stop the destructive chain of events.

7. Responses will vary. Students should use at least one example from the play to support their ideas. Sample responses follow.

   **a.** Hecate's words are the most foreboding because they suggest that Macbeth will meet a miserable, deadly end.

   **b.** Macbeth's words are the most foreboding because they suggest that Macbeth and his wife will commit more horrible crimes.

   **c.** Lennox's words are the most foreboding because they describe a stirring conflict between the people and their king that is bound to end in a bloody struggle.

ANSWER KEY

**d.** Lady Macbeth's words are the most foreboding because she implies that it is better for her and Macbeth to be dead than to be tormented by guilt.

## Written Response

8. Responses will vary. In a model response, students should fulfill the following criteria:

   • demonstrate understanding of the prompt
   • present an imaginary conversation between the ghost of Banquo and Macbeth
   • describe Banquo—in dialogue or narration—either giving Macbeth advice or chastising him for arranging Banquo's murder
   • describe Macbeth—in dialogue or narration—reacting to Banquo's words
   • use quotation marks for dialogue
   • invent dialogue and narration that are consistent with the characters' actions and personalities

---

## Graphic Organizer for Active Reading, Act IV

Responses will vary. Sample responses follow.

### Graphic Organizer

*Good*—Ross (is loyal to Macduff, his family, and their country), Malcolm (reviles Macbeth and mourns his country's fate), Macduff (is horrified by the murders; is ready to fight to the death).

*Evil*—Macbeth (murders without guilt), the witches (delight in evil), the murderers (ruthlessly kill not only Lady Macduff and her children but also every servant).

1. Macbeth and Lady Macbeth have been on the evil side of the moral struggle in the play all along. Ross, Lennox, and Macduff used to be on Macbeth's side even though they were suspicious of him. Malcolm has been on the good side of the struggle since his father's murder. The witches and murderers are forces of evil throughout the play.

2. Guidelines for responses: Most students will think that Macbeth has gone too far to be able to win back his subjects' trust. Events are too suspicious for the situation to be otherwise: Macbeth becomes king after Duncan is murdered; Duncan's sons flee after Macbeth becomes king; and Macbeth sees a ghost after

Banquo's murder. The murders also continue after Duncan's sons flee the country, which makes his sons unlikely suspects for the king's murder. Students who think Macbeth can still win back his subjects should give examples of how Macbeth could do so.

## Making Meanings, Act IV

### Reviewing the Text

**a.** Poisoned entrails, a toad that has been secreting venom through its skin for thirty-one days and was caught when asleep; a slice from a snake that lived in the swamp; eye of newt; toe of frog; wool of bat; tongue of dog; the forked tongue of an adder; a blindworm's sting; a lizard's leg; an owl's wing; dragon's scales; wolf's tooth; witch's mummy; both the gullet and the stomach of a shark; hemlock root dug in the dark; a Jew's liver; goat's gall; slips of yew taken during a lunar eclipse; a Turk's nose, a Tartar's lips; fingers of a baby strangled during birth by its umbilical cord and delivered in a ditch by a prostitute; a tiger's entrails; and the blood of a baboon. Perhaps the witches are putting a spell on Macbeth. Perhaps it is to show how evil the witches are.

**b.** The witches stop him from voicing his question, but he seems to want to know whether he will remain in power (Scene 1, lines 69–70). He also wants to know whether Banquo's issue will ever rule. The witches let the apparitions answer with prophecies and show him a procession of kings (Banquo's descendants).

**c.** First, a helmeted head warns him about Macduff. Second, a bloody child says, "none of woman born / Shall harm Macbeth." Third, a crowned child holding a tree prophesies that Macbeth will never be conquered till Birnam Wood comes to Dunsinane.

**d.** He plans to murder Macduff, but Macduff has fled to England.

**e.** He vows to kill Macduff's family; those family members found at Fife are murdered.

**f.** Scotland has fallen into great distress, with many new widows, orphans, and sorrows.

**g.** He claims to be lustful, greedy, and bent on using power to create chaos.

**h.** He says that the first two (lust and avarice) can be accommodated, but he denounces Malcolm after his last confession (criminality).

### First Thoughts

1. Responses will vary. Sample response: This is becoming ridiculous; what can Macbeth possi-

*Drama Study Guide: The Tragedy of Macbeth*

**108**

HRW MATERIAL COPYRIGHTED UNDER NOTICE APPEARING EARLIER IN THIS WORK.

bly gain from killing Macduff's family? Most students will feel that Macbeth has changed from heroic to evil. Macbeth has sunk to the depths of evil—killing grown men is one thing, but killing innocent children is another.

## Shaping Interpretations

2. The prophecy has been fulfilled by Macbeth. When the witches first see him, he is a hero returning from battle, having saved his nation from a traitor. Now he is a murderer and traitor himself—he has betrayed his country and his honor.

3. Responses will vary. Sample responses: Yes, I think they are responsible for setting in motion the train of evil. Macbeth resists as best he can, but fate (or the spell of the witches) overcomes him. No, I think Macbeth chooses to act of his own free will. There is no evidence in the play that he has been forced, and I think he is actually planning to murder Duncan before he ever sees the witches.

4. It shows Macbeth that not only will Banquo's issue rule, but Banquo's descendants will provide the country with a succession of kings.

5. Responses will vary. Sample responses: Lady Macduff is loyal, good, protective, worried, loving. The boy is clever, knows the Bible well, is loyal and brave.

6. Lady Macduff calls him a traitor for abandoning his family. The murderers mean that he is a traitor to the king (Macbeth). Students will probably agree that Macduff is not a traitor in either sense.

7. He tests Macduff's loyalty—this shows that he is more savvy than his too-trusting father.

## Extending the Text

8. Responses will vary. Some students will feel that a leader represents the nation's status and collective well-being; others will say one person cannot represent so many individuals.

## Challenging the Text

9. *Evaluation:* Responses will vary. Sample responses: No, it is the step that takes Macbeth beyond the pale; it should be seen and acknowledged. Yes, it should be left to the audience's imagination. Without it, the play might lose the immediacy and audience involvement in wanting Macbeth destroyed. The gain would be that the audience would not feel so distraught.

# Literary Elements Worksheet, Act IV

## Understanding Characterization

1. Macbeth's visit to the witches reveals his superstitions, curiosity, and insecurity. He becomes very demanding as he commands the witches to show him the future and is angered at the idea that Banquo will be the father of a line of kings. His ordering the murder of the Macduff family reveals the decline of his moral character and conscience.

2. His words reveal that he is determined to remain king regardless of what heartless actions he will have to perform.

3. a. Malcolm says that Macbeth is treacherous, false, deceitful, and capable of every kind of sin (Scene 3, lines 57–60).

   b. Macduff calls Macbeth a devil and a tyrant (Scene 3, lines 56 and 104).

4. Responses will vary. Perhaps Macbeth's moral and emotional character has declined to the point that he feels he no longer needs a companion to support his actions.

## Applying Skills

Responses will vary. Students should note that in Act I, Macbeth contemplates the murder of Duncan and tries to talk himself out of it. In Act IV, Macbeth no longer has a conscience about his actions but merely conceives an idea and executes it without any sense of compassion.

# Test, Act IV

## Thoughtful Reading

1. b    2. c    3. a    4. c    5. a

## Expanded Response

6. Responses will vary. Students should use at least one example from the play to support their ideas. Answers **a, b, c,** and **d** are all supportable. Sample responses follow.

   a. Macbeth arouses the most sympathy because he is flawed; his weaknesses are exploited by the witches, who use supernatural powers to lure him into doing evil.

   b. Lady Macduff arouses the most sympathy because she is an innocent victim.

   c. Macduff's son arouses the most sympathy because he is killed for his father's flight even though he is only a child and is not actively involved in the conflict.

*Drama Study Guide: The Tragedy of Macbeth*

HRW MATERIAL COPYRIGHTED UNDER NOTICE APPEARING EARLIER IN THIS WORK.

**109**

**d.** Macduff arouses the most sympathy because he loses his family and feels that his flight is the reason for their murders.

**7.** Responses will vary. Sample responses follow.

*An Armed Head—What Might Happen—*Macduff will kill Macbeth. *Why?*—The helmet implies battle; the apparition says to beware of Macduff.

*A Bloody Child—What Might Happen—*Macbeth will kill a child, or an animal or a natural disaster will kill Macbeth, since no one born of a woman will harm Macbeth. *Why?*—The blood implies death; the apparition tells Macbeth he won't be harmed by anyone born of a woman.

*A Crowned Child with a Tree in His Hand—What Might Happen—*A child from Great Birnam Wood will gain the throne. *Why?*—The crown implies a ruler; the tree implies Great Birnam Wood; the apparition tells Macbeth he will be vanquished.

### Written Response

**8.** Responses will vary. In a model response, students should fulfill the following criteria:
- demonstrate understanding of the prompt
- briefly compare Macbeth in Act IV to Macbeth at the beginning of the play
- explain where Macbeth's moral character is on a scale of good to evil
- support their ideas with Macbeth's words or deeds. For example:
  - At the beginning of the play, Macbeth hesitates to kill Duncan and then is tormented by the murder of the king; yet in Act IV, Macbeth coldly decides without hesitation to kill Macduff.
  - Early in the play the mere sight of blood disturbs Macbeth, yet in Act IV he easily decides to slaughter Macduff's wife, children, and any other heirs.

# Graphic Organizer for Active Reading, Act V

Responses will vary. Sample responses follow.

## Graphic Organizer

*First Apparition—Prediction—*Be on guard against Macduff (the Thane of Fife). *How*

*Prediction Comes True—*Macduff kills Macbeth in combat.

*Second Apparition—Prediction—*No one born of a woman will hurt Macbeth. *How Prediction Comes True—*Macduff was delivered by Caesarean section, so he was not, in a sense, born of a woman.

*Third apparition—Prediction—*Macbeth will not be conquered until Birnam Wood comes to Dunsinane Hill. *How Prediction Comes True—*The English troops approach carrying branches from Birnam Wood, giving the appearance that Birnam Wood is approaching Dunsinane Hill.

**1.** Macbeth reacts with panic and despair. When his servant says that Great Birnam Wood appears to be moving, Macbeth calls him a liar and panics. He relies on the second apparition's prophecy to convince himself that Macduff cannot kill him, and then he despairs when Macduff reveals how he was born.

**2.** Most students will state that Macbeth increases his anguish by insisting that the witches reveal his fate. Macbeth's knowledge of his fate causes him to scramble hopelessly to both fulfill and change his fate. Ironically, his very knowledge of his fate is part of his fate. If Macbeth had asked the witches nothing, he might have saved himself much anguish.

# Making Meanings, Act V

### Reviewing the Text

**a.** Her mind is "infected" with evil; she has a guilty conscience.

**b.** He is a tyrant, mad, and a murderer.

**c.** She dies during Scene 5, when the enemy is approaching.

**d.** In Scene 5, lines 2–7, he plans to let the attackers besiege the castle and then drive them home. This is because the castle is strong and he has lost troops (they have defected to help Malcolm). In Scene 5, lines 51–52, he decides to fight because he fears fate is against him yet feels protected by the second apparition's prophecy.

**e.** He has forgotten what it is like to fear; he is sick of life.

**f.** Life is brief, dreary, and meaningless; it is like a brief candle, a poor actor who plays his part and exits from the stage, a story that an idiot tells—noisy, but without meaning.

**g.** Macduff kills Macbeth. Macduff was not born but was ripped from his mother's womb (removed by surgery, not delivered through the birth canal). Birnam Wood comes to Dunsinane as the army uses branches to disguise its advance.

h. Macbeth has been killed and beheaded by Macduff; just as Duncan planned, Malcolm takes the throne.

## First Thoughts

1. Responses will vary. Students may pity Macbeth and be repulsed by the violence, or they may feel that he deserves such a death.

## Shaping Interpretations

2. It emphasizes how she has changed—she has been the cool, collected planner protecting Macbeth from betraying himself. Now she betrays herself and him unawares. Perhaps her sleepwalking represents the sleep disturbance they both endure. It is an effective way to play on the theme of Macbeth's murdering sleep.

3. (Some critics think "one: two" is the clock striking and not a reference to Duncan's death.) The washing of hands and donning of nightgown refer to the night of Duncan's murder. The Thane of Fife's wife refers to the murder of Lady Macduff. The burial of Banquo picks up on Macbeth's strange behavior at the banquet. The knocking at the gate refers to the morning after Duncan's murder.

4. Night and day may stand for tyranny and freedom or for evil and good. The remark foreshadows the outcome of the play by hinting that Macbeth will, in the end, be defeated.

5. Responses will vary. Sample responses: Macbeth's death is the climax; it is the moment when his problems are resolved. The climax occurs when Macduff reveals that he was ripped from his mother's womb; since this fulfills the second apparition's prophecy, Macbeth knows that he is doomed.

6. Responses may vary. The "Tomorrow, and tomorrow, and tomorrow" soliloquy shows Macbeth's resignation. The "I will not yield" speech, before Macbeth fights Macduff to the death, shows that he wants to face death bravely.

## Connecting with the Text

7. Responses will vary. Sample responses: As the play ended, I felt that nothing we do in life is permanent or leaves a lasting mark. I believe there is much meaning to be found in life, and a person can make a difference in the world.

## Challenging the Text

8. *Evaluation.* Responses will vary. Sample responses: It would make her seem more like Macbeth: She, too, sees ghosts and is vulnerable, and sensitivity would become more of a theme; it might make the other ghosts seem more real because Macbeth would not be the only person to see a ghost and treat it as real; the scene might focus too much attention on Lady Macbeth, it might add to the audience's understanding of her demise, or it might seem undignified.

# Elements of Literature Mini-Lesson, Act V

Responses will vary. Possible responses follow.

1. a. In Scene 2, Macbeth reports that someone cried out "Murder" while asleep and that he heard a voice accusing him of murdering sleep. Scene 3 includes the knocking that unnerves the Macbeths. Lennox's speech (Scene 3, lines 52–59) chronicles the night's unusual weather and events, as does the dialogue between Ross and the Old Man (Scene 4, lines 1–20). These images make the mood eerie in order to reflect the unnatural act of murder.

   b. Students may say that the scenes are creepy, disturbing, strange. Unnatural images include the attending toad, the strange comments regarding sailing in a sieve and taking a pilot's thumb, appearances and disappearances into thin air, the horrific ingredients for the brew.

2. a. Sleep is something that weights the eyelid.

   b. Sleep is a knitter, a bath, a balm, and food.

3. *Blood*—Act II, Scene 1, lines 45–49; Scene 3, lines 109–114; Act III, Scene 4, lines 122–126.

   *Darkness*—Act I, Scene 5, lines 49–53; Act II, Scene 4, lines 5–10; Act III, Scene 2, lines 46–53.

   *Disease*—Act IV, Scene 3, lines 141–145; Act V, Scene 1, lines 69–71; Scene 3, lines 37–45.

   *Planting*—Act I, Scene 4, lines 28–29; Act IV, Scene 1, lines 58–61; Act V, Scene 8, lines 64–65.

   Answers regarding the emotional effects of each speech will vary.

# How to Own a Word Mini-Lesson, Act V

## Try It Out

Maps will vary but should follow the example.

*Drama Study Guide: **The Tragedy of Macbeth***

# Language Link Worksheet, Act V

## Exercise A

| 1. A | 2. P | 3. A | 4. A | 5. P |
|------|------|------|------|------|
| 6. P | 7. A | 8. P | 9. A | 10. A |

## Exercise B

1. The witches think their brew to be a powerful mixture.

2. The apparition tells Macbeth not to worry until Birnam Wood comes to Dunsinane.

3. Macbeth sends the murderers to kill the family of Macduff.

4. Malcolm claims that sinful passions, lust, and avarice rule him.

5. Macduff's professions of loyalty comfort Malcolm.

## Exercise C

Revisions will vary. A sample revision follows.

Shakespeare wrote several great tragedies. One of them, *Macbeth,* he wrote in 1606. He loosely based this play on historical events. In *Macbeth,* as in his other tragedies, Shakespeare explored the problems of character, morality, and free will.

*Macbeth* is a powerful play, and its messages are still relevant today. The reader may ponder many questions: Why do Macbeth and Lady Macbeth desire power? Why and how do events change people? How do criminals live with the terrible crimes they commit? The answers to such questions can assist the reader in understanding not only the play but also some current events.

# Literary Elements Worksheet, Act V

## Understanding Elements of the Play

1. The witches' prophecy plants in Macbeth's mind the seed of the idea of becoming king.

2. Duncan's murder is unnatural in that Macbeth is murdering his guest, his kinsman, and his benefactor, in addition to murdering the king.

3. After the murder, Macbeth and Lady Macbeth are unable to sleep. Banquo's murder is another unnatural act. The appearance of Banquo's ghost is certainly not natural. The apparitions Macbeth witnesses and the prophecies they offer are either supernatural or unnatural. The slaughter of Macduff's family is against nature.

Lady Macbeth commits the ultimate unnatural act: suicide.

4. The natural order is restored by Malcolm's accession to the throne as his murdered father's rightful heir. It is accomplished when Macduff avenges the murder of his family by beheading Macbeth.

## Applying Skills

If the theme is that every moral decision has its consequences, the concept of chaos and unnatural events following a disruption of the natural order only underscores that theme.

## Reader's Response

Responses will vary.

# Test, Act V

## Thoughtful Reading

| 1. c | 2. d | 3. b | 4. a | 5. c |
|------|------|------|------|------|

## Expanded Response

6. Responses will vary. Students should use at least one example from the play to support their ideas. All answers are supportable. Sample responses follow.

   a. The mood of the quotation is ambivalent—Siward expresses sorrow at some deaths, but his regret is overshadowed by his conviction of the rightness of the deaths.

   b. The mood of this quotation is happy—Macbeth's death is liberating, and the future is optimistic.

   c. The mood of this quotation is anxiety and regret—Malcolm is worried about the fate of the other men.

   d. The mood of this quotation is jubilation and gratitude—Malcolm is grateful to his loyal subjects and anticipates a joyful coronation.

7. Responses may vary. A sample response follows.

   Macbeth (**c**) is terrified by Macduff's admission that he was "ripped" from his mother's womb. Lady Macbeth (**a** and **d**) is insane and is tormented by her boundless guilt. Macduff (**b**) is enraged and vengeful.

## Written Response

8. Responses will vary. In a model response, students should fulfill the following criteria:

   • demonstrate understanding of the prompt

*Drama Study Guide: The Tragedy of Macbeth*

- choose Lady Macbeth, Young Siward, or Macbeth, and describe the circumstances of his or her death. For example:
  - Lady Macbeth kills herself because she is driven mad by her guilt; Macbeth hears women wailing over her death, and then Seyton tells him the queen is dead.
  - Young Siward dies a noble death; he is slain while fighting and is an admired, fearless soldier.
  - Macduff slays Macbeth in the field after revealing that he, Macduff, was "untimely" taken from his mother's womb.
- explain why the death was or was not inevitable. For example:
  - Lady Macbeth probably would have died by Macbeth's hand if not by her own; she likely would have begun confessing to everyone to assuage her guilt.
  - Young Siward—it seems inevitable that the Earl of Northumberland, who remains unscathed until the very end of the play, will suffer as well by losing his son.
  - Macbeth—it seems that every element of the play leads to Macbeth's inevitable death. He has committed crimes against nature as well as against human beings; Shakespeare's many references to agitation in the supernatural and natural worlds make clear that powerful forces will ensure Macbeth's demise.

# Making Meanings, the Play as a Whole

## Shaping Interpretations

1. Macbeth also did the country a service by dying after he had become tyrannical and evil. In real life sometimes convicted murderers repent or at least apologize.

2. Responses will vary. Sample responses: The ending of the play shows the closing of the circle: Malcolm was named Duncan's heir; Malcolm becomes king, and order is restored, so justice triumphs; good overcomes evil. Since I believe that Macbeth has no choice in his actions, I believe that the play shows evil overcoming good; the return of the good king (Malcolm) will be temporary, for he, too, can be corrupted by powers greater than his resistance.

3. Shakespeare makes Macbeth's fall into evil believable because we can see the mental process by which he begins doing worse and worse deeds. Sample responses: I felt sorry that he gives in to murderous impulses, for he has the potential to be good. I began losing sympathy once he killed Duncan, who had wished Macbeth well.

4. Macbeth does retain some of his original strengths—such as courage in battle, ambition, imagination—but we see how he turns them to evil use. The courage he shows on the battlefield is what allows him to quickly become used to killing off the battlefield. His concern about others' opinions is what keeps him noble (Act I, Scene 7, lines 32–35), but concern about Lady Macbeth's opinion of him makes him give in.

5. Responses will vary. Sample responses: One of the grooms awakens in time to avert Macbeth's murder of Duncan; Banquo warns the king of the witches' prophecies and his concern about Macbeth's interest in these predictions, so that Duncan is on guard.

6. Internal conflicts—ambition versus morality and honesty versus deception in the murders of Duncan and Banquo. External conflicts—between Macbeth and Banquo as Macbeth worries that Banquo's descendants will unthrone him; between Macbeth and Macduff as Macduff appears to distrust Macbeth. In the end, both Macbeths suffer the consequences of guilty consciences due to the internal conflicts, and Macduff ultimately kills Macbeth, clearing the way for Banquo's descendants to rule.

## Extending the Text

7. *Synthesis.* Responses will vary. Students may mention a variety of modern tyrants and dictators: Napoleon, Adolf Hitler, Joseph Stalin, Ferdinand Marcos, or Manuel Noriega; such leaders may be like Macbeth in appearing harsh or having human frailties but unlike Macbeth in specific circumstances. Responses to the question about a tragic hero will vary; remind students to refer to the definition of a tragic hero.

## Challenging the Text

8. *Evaluation.* Responses will vary. Sample response: Yes, parody is a good reminder not to take ourselves or our literary idols too seriously. No, writers should not make fun of a well-written piece of literature that teaches worthwhile lessons about human nature.

*Drama Study Guide: The Tragedy of Macbeth*

HRW MATERIAL COPYRIGHTED UNDER NOTICE APPEARING EARLIER IN THIS WORK.

113

ANSWE

# Choices: Building Your Portfolio, the Play as a Whole

## Critical Writing

1. Ask students to cite specific references to or speeches by Lady Macbeth and to discuss why Shakespeare might have included particular words or actions and what these words or actions suggest.

## Critical Writing

2. Before students begin writing, have them review Macbeth's speeches to look for places in the play in which he uses the same techniques as the witches (equivocation, deceit through ambiguity). This will allow them to see the question in a broader perspective.

## Oral Interpretation

3. Suggest that students experiment with various readings to find the most effective pitch, tempo, volume, and pace. Ask them to recopy the speech in large, readable letters and to make notations as to which places require pauses or emphasis.

## Critical Thinking/Speaking

4. Encourage students to consider the witnesses carefully. Possibilities include Banquo's ghost, one of the witches, the gentlewoman who attends Lady Macbeth, the doctor, and Seyton. Suggest that the two teams work together at first so that they will be aware of and able to respond to all the evidence the other side will present.

## Creative Writing

5. Students' parodies will vary. Make sure students understand that parody involves more than merely flinging abuse at another writer. Wise parodists use imitation as a tool to better understand a work.

## Critical Thinking

6. Students' responses will vary, although certain scenes will recur often, such as Duncan's and Banquo's murders and Lady Macbeth's sleepwalking. It is best for students to choose a small section of the scene to work with so they can pay careful attention to the language.

## Critical Thinking

7. Most students will probably think that Macbeth would be assured a place in Dante's Hell. Not only does he commit multiple murders, but he betrays his close friends and the king, to whom he has pledged loyalty. Brutus, Cassius, and Judas, the three "worst" sinners in the Inferno, were traitors as well.

# Test, the Play as a Whole

## Responding to Literature

1. Responses will vary. A sample follows.

   *Character*—Macbeth

   *Options*—After the witch tells Macbeth that he is destined to be king, he can either be content with his current position as Thane of Glamis and wait for the throne, or he can murder the king and possibly accelerate his rise to the throne.

   *Decision*—Macbeth decides to kill the king.

2. Responses will vary. A sample follows.

   *Contributions*—The images of nature in revolt contribute to the sense of chaos, foreboding, and violence. This physical environment reflects the mental and emotional environment of the characters.

   *Contributions*—Macbeth describes Banquo and Fleance as serpents, thereby contributing to the atmosphere of danger. His description of Fleance as one who will become venomous contributes to the theme of the continuing growth of evil.

3. Responses will vary. In a model response, students should fulfill the following criteria:
   - demonstrate understanding of the prompt
   - provide an interpretation of Lennox's comment. For example:
     - When Lennox makes his comment in Act III, Macbeth controls the country—it is in the "palm of his hand." His hand is cursed according to the witches' prophecies and due to the blood he has spilled and the chaos he has created. (The image of the cursed hand is applied to Lady Macbeth, too; the passages about her fruitless efforts to wash blood from her hands are some of the most famous in the play.)
   - explain how the quotation relates to the events, characters, and theme of the play. For example:
     - An accursed hand seems to govern every event in the play. At the beginning of *Macbeth,* it may be the cursed hand of fate that steers Macbeth into the witches' path. The characters in the play suffer at

*Drama Study Guide: The Tragedy of Macbeth*

either the bloody hands of Macbeth or the cruel hand of fate, or both. One theme of the play—that it might be better to abandon the idea of free will—assumes that the hand of fate is omnipotent.

- support their ideas with references to the play (previous examples are sufficient)

4. Responses will vary. In a model response, students should fulfill the following criteria:
   - demonstrate understanding of the prompt
   - define a tragic hero. For example:
     - A tragic hero is usually a dignified, courageous, and high-ranking character who suffers defeat and, possibly, death. The tragic hero usually gains self-knowledge and wisdom during his or her struggles.
   - support their ideas with at least two references to the play. For example:
     - At the beginning of the play, Macbeth is a nobleman. In recognition of his success on the battlefield, he is named Thane of Cawdor by the king.
     - As the play progresses, Macbeth changes from a good man to a man deluded by his greed for power. His many crimes inevitably lead to catastrophe, including his own death.

# Testing the Genre

## Understanding Vocabulary

**1.** c **2.** a **3.** b **4.** a **5.** d

## Thoughtful Reading

**6.** c **7.** b **8.** a **9.** c **10.** d

## Expanded Response

11. Responses will vary. Students should use at least one example from the excerpt to support their ideas. Guidelines for evaluating responses:
    a. Students should recognize that Hamlet has been convinced of the king's guilt and has decided that it is his duty to revenge his father's death. In the excerpted speech, he deliberates on the proper moment to enact his revenge (lines 54–60). Hamlet wants to make sure Claudius's soul winds up in hell and thus hesitates to kill him when he is praying (lines 38–43 and 49–53).
    b. Students may say that the fact that Hamlet does not show himself directly to the king

but instead eavesdrops on him points to a cunning nature. So, too, might the fact that Hamlet thinks about killing Claudius while the king's back is turned (lines 38–39). His decision to kill the king while he is sinning (lines 54–60) shows that Hamlet is a clever thinker, and cleverness is often associated with cunning.

c. Many students will think that Hamlet's change of mind points to a hesitation on his part. The questions that he voices might give the speech a hesitant tone (lines 45–47 and 48–51). The fact that he has his sword drawn and then sheaths it is visual evidence of hesitation (line 53).

d. His emphatic "No," which takes up an entire line, is proof that Hamlet has a decisive nature, as is the fact that he ends the speech by deciding on a definite course of action—killing Claudius while he is sinning and sparing his mother's life (lines 54–60).

## Written Response

12. Responses will vary. In a model response, students should fulfill the following criteria:
    - demonstrate understanding of the prompt
    - clearly compare and contrast Macbeth's and Hamlet's motives for regicide.
    - support their ideas with at least two examples from both *Macbeth* and the excerpt from *Hamlet*. For example:
      - Each is goaded on by another: Macbeth is encouraged by his wife, and Hamlet by the ghost of his father. In the excerpt, Hamlet considers his father's dire predicament (lines 45–49).
      - Hamlet kills the king for a noble reason, to revenge his father's death (lines 38–44 and 49–52), whereas Macbeth commits regicide merely for personal gain.
      - Duncan, Macbeth's victim, has done nothing wrong, but Claudius, Hamlet's victim, is guilty of regicide, as well as fratricide, and Hamlet has proof of this. In the excerpt, the audience hears Claudius confess his guilt (lines 1–5).

# English Language Worksheet

## Shakespeare's Language

**1.** c **2.** b **3.** d **4.** b **5.** c
**6.** c **7.** c **8.** b **9.** c **10.** d

*Drama Study Guide: The Tragedy of Macbeth*

HRW MATERIAL COPYRIGHTED UNDER NOTICE APPEARING EARLIER IN THIS WORK.

**115**

# TEACHING NOTES

# TEACHING NOTES

# TEACHING NOTES

# TEACHING NOTES

# TEACHING NOTES

# TEACHING NOTES

# TEACHING NOTES

# TEACHING NOTES